Dr Aparna Rao is a distinguished criminal barrister at 5 Paper Buildings, London, specialising in complex criminal and civil fraud. She is known for her adept handling of intricate legal matters, often involving financial, technical, or evidentially complex issues. She combines this to great effect with her straightforward and incisive manner which inspires confidence in clients and courts. Her expertise and flair makes her a sought-after junior in large fraud cases.

Her impressive academic credentials include undergraduate degrees in Law and Science at the Australian National University in Canberra. She then qualified as a lawyer in 2009 and worked as an Associate to a Justice of the High Court of Australia (the final appellate court in Australia, the equivalent of the UK Supreme Court). She taught as a Lecturer in Law at the Australian National University, and later tutored in Law at Oxford University while completing her Doctorate in Law. Her doctoral thesis focused on the bad character of the defendant in criminal trials.

In 2013, Aparna cross-qualified and was called to the Bar of England and Wales.

Aparna has a very successful practice defending in disciplinary and regulatory proceedings in the healthcare and policing sectors. She is instructed in MTIC and fraud-related proceedings in the VAT Tribunal. She sits as a part-time judge in the Employment Tribunal and the First-tier Tribunal.

A Practical Guide to Bad Character Evidence for Criminal Practitioners

Second Edition

A Practical Guide to Bad Character Evidence for Criminal Practitioners

Second Edition

Aparna Rao
DPhil, MPhil, BCL (Oxon)
LLB (Hons), BSc (ANU)
Barrister (Middle Temple)

Law Brief Publishing

Published 2025 by Law Brief Publishing, an imprint of Law Brief Publishing Ltd
30 The Parks
Minehead
Somerset
TA24 8BT

www.lawbriefpublishing.com

Paperback: 978-1-916698-97-0

For those who make this worthwhile

FOREWORD

In stories told to children throughout the ages, protagonists commonly divide into individuals of good character and those of bad character. So it is no surprise that, when adult members of a jury are called upon to decide whether they are sure that a person is guilty of an offence with which they have been charged, they may recall the stories they heard as children and wonder about that person's character. After all, how a person has behaved in the past may seem like a reliable guide to how they behave today.

This is sometimes called the narrative fallacy: a form of biased thinking which leads us to interpret real events as we once understood stories, with coherent chains of cause and effect, helping us to make sense of the world. But storytelling is a poor guide to the truth, and real human lives are richer, messier, and more complex.

For those of us who spend most of our professional time in the area of civil justice, we must make conscious efforts not to fall into the trap of the narrative fallacy when we assess the evidence we have heard. In the field of criminal justice, however, liberty is often at stake. More safeguards are needed. Accordingly, the law strictly regulates what a jury may be told about what a person's previous behaviour. In this way, juries are supported in making objective assessments of the evidence, resisting the natural inclination to form views based on what a defendant may have said or done in the past.

In the second edition of her excellent book, Aparna Rao expertly guides us through the complex legal framework that governs the admissibility of evidence of bad character. Her book is concise, resolutely practical, and accessibly written. This makes it of equal value to students, to busy prosecution and defence practitioners, and to judges required to reach quick decisions on matters of law while the jury is absent. It incorporates recent developments in case law and includes, at the end, a new and helpful checklist of matters to consider. Dr Rao's clear and welcome guide serves the interests of fairness and justice in criminal trials.

Judge Barry Clarke
President of Employment Tribunals (England and Wales)
Visiting Judge of the Employment Appeal Tribunal
Recorder (Crown Court and County Court)
Authorised to sit as a High Court Judge
(King's Bench Division, Administrative Court)

PREFACE TO THE SECOND EDITION

I have been flattered and touched by the positive feedback I received on the first edition of this guide. We all experience the feeling of wondering whether our understanding of the law is generally the same as everyone else's, let alone whether we can explain it well enough to be understood by those who matter in that moment. I am very grateful for many constructive and encouraging responses.

Nothing over the past four years has changed my view that bad character evidence is complicated and pervasive. It needs careful and structured treatment. Since starting to sit in a judicial capacity I have also begun to understand the pressures on judges managing cases and hearing evidence.

Evidential rules are thoroughly practical but also have to reflect the principles that guide them. In principle, a jury is entitled to hear evidence that establishes a propensity to commit a certain kind of offence, but how much evidence is sufficient? What if it is disputed? Who decides what propensity is established? When does that decision happen?

The answers to these questions are not always straightforward.

I looked at some of these questions during three years of research on my PhD into the bad character of the defendant under the Criminal Justice Act 2003. The hundreds of Court of Appeal cases that had been generated during just six years revealed that there was perhaps more than the usual level of confusion over the meaning and implementation of the provisions.

When I came to the Bar a few years later, it quickly became apparent that the words of the statute bear little resemblance to the way bad character evidence is perceived by practitioners and judges. The Court of Appeal decisions I had studied in the abstract for several years suddenly became explicable in a wholly different light. This book is designed to share these explanations in as clear and structured a way as possible.

It would not have been possible for me even to contemplate my studies, my career or this book were it not for the unparalleled support of my family: they know who they are and what they have done for me. My thesis research owes its success to my supervisors, Colin Tapper and Peter Mirfield, authors of the leading texts on the law of Evidence, for whose guidance and patience I am especially grateful.

Heartfelt thanks go to all the lecturers, tutors, professors and other positive influences at the Australian National University and Oxford University, who helped me explore my potential and encouraged my love of research and law.

My colleagues at the bar and my clerks at 5 Paper Buildings are the family I depend on for everything law-related. Several have given up their valuable time to read and comment on drafts of the first edition and this revision. Particular thanks go to Carolina Bracken, Rebecca Penfold, HHJ Andrew Johnson, and Felix Tambling. All errors remaining are entirely my own.

The stated law is believed to be correct and up to date as at 1st May 2025. Please do check for updates to the law and in particular to any rules / practice directions.

Dr Aparna Rao
May 2025

CONTENTS

TABLE OF CASES

TABLE OF LEGISLATION

CHAPTER ONE

INTRODUCTION

A defining characteristic of the criminal law is the way in which its rules of evidence fundamentally change the facts of a case.

This is because of the unique role of the jury: it is the sole arbiter of facts, but has no say in the law that governs what evidence it is given in order to determine the facts. There are sound reasons for this. Our criminal justice system relies on transparency, consistency, and fairness being done and seen to be done. The law is often not easy to comprehend and apply. We therefore leave this task to the lawyers. The resulting factual matrix, achieved after application of the law of evidence, is used by the jury to reach a verdict.

Whether bad character evidence will be used is a question asked in all cases that are expected to proceed to trial. It is natural to draw inferences about a person from known facts or assertions. We all know how easy it is instantly to form a view about another person from a profession, hobby, mannerism or speech. But the criminal justice process relies on the making of objective assessments of another person without reference to personal prejudice.

The human ability to control prejudices and make objective assessments has often proved inadequate. Parliament has taken the view that people who determine the facts in a criminal trial need assistance in order to achieve objective assessments. Thus, the natural inclination to make inferences from evidence about a person's character is now regulated.

At common law, evidence from which inferences about the bad character of the defendant can be drawn was generally called 'similar fact evidence'. After reports from the Criminal Law Revision Committee (CLRC) in

1972 and the Law Commission in 1996 and 2001,[1] Parliament enacted the Criminal Justice Act 2003 Part 11 Chapter 1 ('CJA'), which came into force on 15 December 2004.[2]

Since the first edition of this guide, the landscape of criminal evidence has continued to evolve in both judicial interpretation and practical application. In the four years since the first edition of this text, the Court of Appeal (Criminal Division) has considered bad character as a ground of appeal against conviction in no fewer than 200 cases. That is a large proportion of total conviction appeals between October 2020 and September 2023[3] (approximately 500).

As always, the aim of this work is to make it easier for practitioners, students, and users of the criminal justice system to navigate this complex and important area. This second edition offers a refined analysis that reflects recent developments and enhanced practical guidance.

The CJA's purpose is to aid juries in making objective assessments by regulating the natural inclination to form judgments based on a defendant's character. There is new guidance on evolving topics:

- gang-related bad character,
- additions to the types of non-conviction bad character evidence

---

1 *Evidence of Bad Character in Criminal Proceedings* (Law Com No 273, 2001).

2 This text deals with ss.98-112. Section 113 gives effect to a Schedule of amendments concerning the armed forces, an area outside the scope of this book.

3 The last available annual review data at the time of publication, so this figure is short by 1 year's data.

- non-defendant bad character, especially the making of false allegations,

- giving a false impression and correcting it with bad character evidence

- cross-admissibility and the combination direction on both propensity and coincidence

- a suggested checklist for approaching bad character issues

I have also incorporated invaluable feedback from readers who have used the first edition in practice and study. In footnotes you will find references to cases that, while not adding to principle, contain factual scenarios on the relevant issue. Feedback has indicated that looking at similar factual scenarios can assist readers to decide how to deploy evidence in their own cases.

Taking its cue from the legislation itself, this text will normally use male gender-specific pronouns, relying upon the interpretive rule that these actually refer to all genders.

The task of interpreting the CJA is primarily case law based. I have prioritised giving media-neutral citations where possible.

CHAPTER TWO

WHAT IS BAD CHARACTER EVIDENCE?

This Chapter deals with the different types of bad character evidence, from allegations and acquittals to cautions and foreign convictions. It examines how s.98(a) and s.109 operate, the effect of s.74 of the Police and Criminal Evidence Act 1984 ('PACE'), the meaning of relevance, and how to give notice or apply to admit bad character evidence. Good character and appropriate directions are also examined.

"*Bad character*" is defined as evidence of, or of a disposition towards, misconduct.

"98 'Bad character'

References in this Chapter to evidence of a person's 'bad character' are to evidence of, or of a disposition towards, misconduct on his part, other than evidence which—

> *(a) has to do with the alleged facts of the offence with which the defendant is charged, or*
>
> *(b) is evidence of misconduct in connection with the investigation or prosecution of that offence."*

Section 112 defines "*misconduct*" by the following closed definition: "*'misconduct' means the commission of an offence or other reprehensible behaviour.*"

In the context of gateway (g), the definition of 'character' when referring to another person's character is technically different from that of 'bad character' as defined in ss 98 and 112(1). Section 106(2) gives an exclusive, closed definition of evidence that attacks another person's character.

However, in essence it is very similar to 'bad character' because it is evidence "*to the effect*" that someone has committed an offence or has behaved, or is disposed to behave, in a reprehensible way.[1]

2.1 "The Commission Of An Offence"

This is straightforward. If the defendant has a conviction from England and Wales recorded against him on his Police National Computer record ('PNC'), this is evidence of bad character. Note that, technically speaking, the conviction is not *itself* bad character. It is *evidence of* bad character.[2] As examined later in this Chapter, a defendant is entitled to seek to demonstrate that he did not in fact commit the offence.

A finding of dangerousness (during sentencing) is not part of the commission of the offence.[3]

A spent conviction is, nonetheless, evidence of the commission of an offence. The fact that it is spent may, depending on the statutory test being applied, be relevant to whether it is admissible.[4]

2.1.1 Foreign Convictions

The general definition does not deal directly with foreign convictions (including Scottish, Northern Irish, and EU ones). However, in terms of gateway (d), s.103(7) explicitly contemplates the use of convictions for an offence under the law of any country outside England and Wales in the context of determining whether two offences are of the same

---

1 See Chapter 4 gateway (g).

2 See *Hussain* [2008] EWCA Crim 1117 and discussion below concerning facts underlying a charge.

3 *Reid* [2024] EWCA Crim 308, [47]. See below on non-conviction bad character evidence.

4 Rehabilitation of Offenders Act 1974, s.7(2)(a).

description or category as required for s.103(2) (as to which see Chapter 4 gateway (d) discussion). Section 108(2A) performs a similar function in relation to comparing a foreign conviction incurred when the defendant was under the age of 14 (see Chapter 5).

As far as the use of foreign convictions under the other gateways and non-defendant bad character is concerned, there is limited case law. Section 103(7) and s.108(2A) provide bespoke rules for specific uses of convictions that arise in those sections. Their wording does not expressly preclude the use of foreign convictions in other ways. The definition of misconduct in s.112(1) is not restricted by jurisdiction. It is likely, therefore, that foreign convictions can be used as evidence of bad character more generally.

Caution should be exercised when ascertaining the accuracy of any record of foreign convictions, and the details of the underlying facts. The onus is on the prosecution; the fact that a defendant may have been present for some or all of the foreign proceedings does not relieve the prosecution of its obligation to obtain suitable evidence and details of the conviction.[5] It can often be difficult to establish sufficient similarity or otherwise of a foreign conviction to a comparable offence or category of offences in England and Wales (especially for propensity-based arguments, where elements of the offending may be particularised differently). However, in *Donnelly* evidence of a French conviction which may have required a different level of knowledge or intent on the part of the defendant was still admissible under gateway (d) as showing a propensity to commit the equivalent offence in England and Wales. Note that the French conviction did not fall under s.103(4)(a) (i.e. was not in the same terms as England and Wales offence), but it qualified under "*any other way*" of showing propensity under s.103(2).[6]

---

5 This, it is unnecessary to say, goes for all bad character evidence whether of foreign extraction or not: see *Humphris* [2005] EWCA Crim 2030.

6 *Donnelly* [2007] EWCA Crim 3360, [15].

Questions of procedural (or even substantive) fairness in a foreign jurisdiction might trigger exclusionary provisions: see, for example, *Brooks*, concerning foreign convictions from France, Spain and Morocco.[7]

If a defendant disputes a conviction, s.74(3) of PACE no longer assists in respect of non-UK convictions. As of 31 December 2020 convictions in EU Member States no longer give rise to the legal presumption that the defendant has committed that offence unless the contrary is proved: s.74(3) of PACE.[8] Presumably, EU convictions are now to be treated like any other non-UK convictions. Where there is no s.74 presumption, and the relevance of the disputed conviction might be diminished to the extent that, bearing in mind the risk of satellite litigation, it ought not to be used.[9]

In *Kordasinski*,[10] the defendant was convicted of rape, assault by penetration, and false imprisonment (acquitted of fourth charge of kidnapping). The question was whether and how the defendant's previous convictions in Poland (2000) were admissible and then provable. The previous convictions were similar in that they were equivalent to domestic convictions for rape, threats with a weapon, and false imprisonment, of two women each in identical but separate circumstances on the same day. The defendant accepted that the convictions established a propensity and so were admissible under gateway (d) and s.103. However, he said that he had been wrongly convicted in Poland, disputing the evidence given there and the Polish criminal procedures and standards of proof. He wished to restrict the admissible evidence to the fact of the convictions only, excluding any details of evidence.

---

7 *Brooks* [2014] EWCA Crim 562. For the exclusionary provisions see Chapter 6.

8 For old cases on s.74 and EU convictions, see *Erhan* [2014] EWCA Crim 1523; *Zawadzka* [2016] EWCA Crim 171; *Reece* [2020] EWCA Crim 44.

9 See *Brooks* [2014] EWCA Crim 562 re the Moroccan conviction.

10 *Kordasinski* [2006] EWCA Crim 2984, [2007] 1 Cr App R 17.

The Court held that:

- The rule in *Hollington v Hewthorn*[11] no longer applies to UK[12] or foreign convictions. Section 99(1) of the CJA abolishes common law rules governing the admissibility of evidence of bad character in criminal proceedings. Section 99(2) and s.118(1) together do not preserve *Hollington v Hewthorn.*[13]

- The Polish convictions were admissible under both gateways (d) (with s.103) and (g).

- Under s.101(3) the details could not fairly have been put before the jury.

As to whether non-conviction foreign bad character can be used, the concerns expressed above as to detail, proof, and satellite litigation will normally be heightened. Their use is not, however, precluded by the wording of the legislation. In *McAllister,*[14] details of an allegation tried in Scotland were admissible in England under gateway (d) to show propensity, notwithstanding that the Scottish jury had returned a verdict of 'not proven'. In *Clifford*, the judge admitted evidence of a complaint said to have taken place in Spain.[15]

---

11 *Hollington v Hewthorn* [1943] 1 KB 587: i.e. that a criminal conviction was not admissible as evidence that the convicted person was guilty of the offence for which he was convicted.

12 By virtue of s.73 of PACE.

13 *Kordasinski* [2006] EWCA Crim 2984, [2007] 1 Cr App R 17, [72].

14 *McAllister* [2008] EWCA Crim 1544, [2009] 1 Cr App R 10.

15 *Clifford* [2014] EWCA Crim 2245, [45]. This was an appeal against sentence; the judgment does not reveal whether the admissibility of the Spain allegation was disputed.

2.2 "Other Reprehensible Behaviour"

By definition, "*other reprehensible behaviour*" means non-conviction evidence.

The CJA does not elaborate on the wide variety of non-conviction incidents that might be covered by "*reprehensible behaviour*".

Examples of things that might be "*other reprehensible behaviour*" include:

- Unproved allegations
- Cautions
- Warnings
- Allegations resulting in acquittals
- Prison adjudications[16]
- A finding that a person did an act (while unfit to plead)[17]
- Statements that indicate the maker's desire or motivation to commit an illegal act: for example lyrics that refer to violent actions and weapons[18]
- Non-criminal findings, such as the outcomes of disciplinary hearings,[19] civil tribunals, county courts

---

16 *Reid* [2024] EWCA Crim 308.

17 *Renda* [2005] EWCA Crim 2826, [2006] 1 Cr App R 24.

18 *Martin* [2017] EWCA Crim 488, [24]; *Palmer* [2016] EWCA Crim 2237, [28]. See below Chapter 4.4.5 on gangs and associations.

19 *Gaiziunas* [2024] EWCA Crim 246 re police misconduct proceedings.

- Disclosures to HMRC of tax fraud under the Code of Practice 9 Facility (COP9)[20]
- Issue of Prohibition Notices and Notices of Contravention in prosecutions for breaches of health and safety law[21]
- A finding of dangerousness for the purposes of sentencing[22]
- Allegations of misconduct in a foreign jurisdiction[23]

The phrase "other reprehensible conduct" invites a moral judgement that is different from simply establishing the fact of a conviction.

As an example, in *Marsh* the defendant was convicted of the murder of his wife (by persuading his girlfriend H to commit the murder, using a

---

20 No case law has been located on the subject. In principle if D has admitted to certain matters during a procedure designed to secure full disclosure and a commitment not to continue the fraudulent activity, in exchange for a promise not to prosecute, it is difficult to see why this information cannot then be used in subsequent criminal proceedings for a similar but *undisclosed* fraud. The position might be different if the new fraud is not one that would need to be reported to HMRC.

21 *Health and Safety Executive v Evergreen Construction UK Ltd* [2023] EWCA Crim 237.

22 This should be approached with extreme caution: *Reid* [2024] EWCA Crim 308, [47]. This finding requires a judge to make an assessment on present evidence of future risk. "*There are obvious difficulties about seeking to justify such an assessment being admissible as evidence of bad character – that is to say, misconduct or other reprehensible behaviour.*"

23 *Kalala* [2024] EWCA Crim 1836: video evidence of D using firearms in Turkey was relevant and admissible. The behaviour was legal in Turkey. Although P did not approach this as bad character evidence, the judge in the alternative found that it was gateway (d) evidence. This was remedied by a good character direction and a direction against propensity reasoning.

knife). H had pleaded guilty and, it appears, gave evidence at the defendant's trial. The bad character evidence was: (i) the defendant's interest in cutting (both of himself and others) as a form of sexual gratification (and evidence of this from former girlfriends); and (ii) in 2005 the defendant had planned to assault someone and, as in the present case, had sought to arrange a false alibi.[24] The interest in cutting was said to be relevant to an important matter in issue: whether the defendant had exercised controlling influence over H to persuade her to carry out the killing. The alibi evidence from 2005 was relevant to "*an issue*"—whether the murder was spontaneous or whether the defendant had planned it and given himself an alibi.[25] There was a "tacit agreement" between application partes that the evidence was admissible, presumably via gateway (a).[26] and did not decide whether it was actually bad character evidence. In directing the jury, the exact relevance of the 2005 evidence and the "*cutting evidence*" was not spelt out, but was, it seems, "clear to the jury".[27] The cutting was reprehensible behaviour because according to societal standards it was abnormal. It is debatable whether it was relevant to any aspect of the case.[28]

In *Joyce* (a Northern Ireland case involving a dispute between members of the travelling community), references to "*bare knuckle fighter*" were bad character, as was the description that the defendant was "*king of the travellers*", because it "*has connotations and links with bare knuckle fighting*".[29]

---

24 An error shows s.100 instead of s.101: *Marsh* [2009] EWCA Crim 2696, [42].

25 *Marsh* [2009] EWCA Crim 2696, [44].

26 *Marsh* [2009] EWCA Crim 2696, [46].

27 *Marsh* [2009] EWCA Crim 2696, [54] and [57].

28 A medical report mentioned on appeal, but not admitted at trial, may have assisted.

29 *Joyce* [2023] NICA 67, [119].

2.2.1 *Unproved Allegations*

Typically, these include:

- Allegations of a similar type to the current charge, e.g. of previous incidents of domestic violence perpetrated by D against C but not charged
- Investigations into earlier behaviour that led to the current charges, but have not been prosecuted
- Pending prosecutions that have not yet come to trial
- Bind-overs are a particularly grey area—they may be evidence of bad character depending on the circumstances.[30] Note the effect on a good character direction (as to which see later in this Chapter)

2.2.1.1 *Satellite Litigation*

There are difficulties associated with treating evidence of an unproved allegation as evidence of bad character. In particular, ascertaining the truth of the allegation (as to this see also Chapter 6 on the standard of proof) and the risk of satellite litigation, might be convincing reasons not to admit mere allegations.[31]

Satellite litigation is a common pitfall and is to be avoided. It can arise in respect of any type of bad character evidence, but is most common in relation to unproved allegations. It consists of the risk that asking the jury to use bad character evidence requires them first to ascertain whether the allegation is true or not. This means the jury are distracted from the

---

30 *B(E)* [2017] EWCA Crim 35, [2017] 1 Cr App R 31, [46] onwards.

31 *Millward* [2008] EWCA Crim 644, [19].

offence on the indictment by needing to consider the satellite litigation of a second accusation.

An egregious instance of this is *O'Dowd*, where the extensive satellite litigation of three disputed allegations was a significant factor in prolonging the trial. The Court observed that:

> *"It is incumbent upon a judge considering the application to try to project forward to see the problems which might later arise in the trial as a result of the disputed bad character evidence being admitted before ruling on the application. This is because, once the evidence is admitted, unless it has been contaminated (and section 107 applies) the question is of its weight. The judge will then only have limited remedies open to deal with problems that arise thereafter."*[32]

The Court in *McKenzie* said that proof of previous alleged misconduct (i.e. not via a conviction) "*requires the trial of a collateral or satellite issue*".[33] This is undesirable and is a powerful argument against the admission of bad character evidence. Before deciding whether and how to admit it, it may be helpful to ask how much additional evidence the satellite litigation will require and how the jury are going to be directed to use it.

One exception to the satellite litigation rule is where bad character evidence is adduced by a co-defendant:

> *"We do have sympathy with the judge's observation that there is a danger that allowing evidence of this kind will give rise to satellite litigation and distract the jury and take their eye off the ball. But it seems to us that, as the rules currently operate, this is not a basis for excluding evidence of bad character when relied on by one accused*

---

32 *O'Dowd* [2009] EWCA Crim 905, [2009] 2 Cr App R 16, [60].

33 *McKenzie* [2008] EWCA Crim 758, [23]. See Chapter 6 on standard and directions.

against another, however desirable it may be to have a rule of that nature."[34]

2.2.1.2 Charges Versus Facts Underlying A Charge

The mere fact that someone has been charged with an offence is not bad character or evidence of bad character.

In *Hussain* (2008)[35] D1 and D2 were both charged with attempted robbery from D1's workplace. D1 said that he acted under duress from D2, and relied upon an incident some eight years ago where D2 was originally tried for murder, but convicted of manslaughter; that conviction was quashed and at retrial D2 pleaded to assault occasioning actual bodily harm.[36] The prosecution successfully relied upon evidence of this conviction for ABH.[37] But D1 wanted, via gateways (c) or (e), to use the fact that D2 had been charged with murder (although not convicted of it), to support the defence that he (D1) had acted under duress.

The Court stated:

- A conviction by itself is not misconduct; it is only "*excellent and very often irrefutable evidence of misconduct.*"[38] This is because it is the misconduct, not the *evidence* of misconduct, that is the bad

---

34 *Apabhai* [2011] EWCA Crim 917, [40].

35 *Hussain* [2008] EWCA Crim 1117.

36 Previous convictions for offences of dishonesty of both defendants had already been admitted via gateway (a). The judge had also admitted, via gateway (e), evidence on behalf of D2 that a witness had seen possible drug transactions taking place at D1's workplace. Neither of these admissions was disputed on appeal.

37 Via gateway (g), because D2 had attacked D1's character by alleging that he supplied drugs.

38 *Hussain* [2008] EWCA Crim 1117, [13].

character (an interpretation based upon the structure of the opening words of s.98). "*It is not unusual to see the concept of bad character wrongly elided with that of conviction.*"

- D2 being charged with murder is not equivalent to D2 committing an act of misconduct. Only the facts that give rise to that charge can amount to misconduct.

- In fact, "*a mere charge, unproved, could not be evidence of bad character, still less could it be bad character itself*".

- Therefore in the present case, "*the only available evidence of misconduct was evidence of a conviction for assault occasioning actual bodily harm. That was the only conviction which had resulted. It proved misconduct to that extent and no further.*"[39]

For a contrasting approach see *W*, where the allegation that a prosecution witness had been "*under investigation for theft*" was bad character evidence.[40]

Even if the fact that being charged with something cannot amount to bad character or evidence of bad character, it is common and accepted practice to use evidence of the *facts that led to* the charge as evidence of bad character. There are many cases in which evidence of an unproved allegation, sometimes the subject of a charge, and sometimes only the subject of another person's accusation, has been permitted to be used as evidence of bad character.

The distinction between the fact of the charge/trial (not bad character) and the evidence underlying it (bad character) is not always maintained: see, for example, *Hobbs*, where the bad character evidence was said to include "*the fact that D2 had been arrested for, and was awaiting trial on*"

39 *Hussain* [2008] EWCA Crim 1117, [14]

40 W [2022] EWCA Crim 1438, [49].

certain matters.[41] In fact, reliance was not placed on the fact of the upcoming trial. The real bad character evidence was the substance of the charges that D2 faced.

In *Hussain* (above), the fact that D2 had been *charged* was not evidence of bad character. Therefore, D1 should have been able to use the fact of the charge without needing to satisfy s.101, to support his *belief* that D2 was a violent man who had a conviction for murder (however mistaken that belief might have been). Evidence that D2 had in the past been tried for murder might help to show that there was some foundation for D1's asserted belief.[42]

If there is a risk of the jury becoming unduly prejudiced on account of the murder allegation, exclusionary provisions may apply (see Chapter 5). Appropriate directions (Chapter 6) should be given if the evidence is nonetheless admissible.

2.2.2 Acquittals, Cautions And Warnings

Acquittals, police cautions, and police warnings are types of bad character evidence that are neither evidence of convictions nor of mere unproved allegations. All can have some characteristics of bad character evidence, but all can also be distinguished from convictions in that they are unlikely to, or cannot, lead to convictions.

2.2.2.1 Evidence Underlying An Acquittal

The facts underlying charges of which a person has actually been acquitted can still be used as bad character evidence. While this may appear to undermine the effect of having been acquitted, both pre- and post-CJA

---

41 *Hobbs* [2018] EWCA Crim 1003, [2018] 2 Cr App R (S) 36, [9].

42 *Hussain* [2008] EWCA Crim 1117, [14]-[15]. However, the conviction was safe because the defence of duress could not properly have succeeded even if this additional piece of evidence had been before the jury.

case law suggest that doing so is permissible.[43] It is, however, by no means inevitable[44] and it carries a high risk of satellite litigation.

That was made clear in *Mustapha*,[45] where D1 was convicted of murder and attempted murder occurring in April 2004. The judge admitted as bad character evidence the fact that D1 was allegedly seen in possession of a gun in a separate event in November 2004. It was not a gun that could have been used in the April murder. The jury were told that D1 had been tried and acquitted in June 2005 of firearms offences arising from this matter. The Court of Appeal said of the use of an acquittal:

> *"it was incumbent on the judge to direct the jury that they could only use this evidence to support the identification of [D1] if they were first sure that [D1] had been carrying a gun when seen by the police officers in November 2004 …"*[46]

The judge attempted to prevent a descent into satellite litigation by cautioning counsel against re-litigating the bad character evidence, but later directed the jury to be "*sure it is proved*" before using that evidence. The Court of Appeal said:

> *"We have no doubt that this evidence was highly prejudicial to [D1] … It arose out of offences of which [D1] had been acquitted. Despite, the judge at the end of his ruling indicating to counsel that he did*

---

43 *Z* [2000] 2 AC 483, [2000] 3 All ER 385; *Al Badi* [2007] EWCA Crim 2974.

44 In *Nguyen* [2008] EWCA Crim 585, [2008] 2 Cr App R 9, had D been tried and acquitted of certain allegations before the current trial, it was not likely that the facts of those allegations would have been left to the jury as evidence of propensity.

45 *Mustapha* [2007] EWCA Crim 1702.

46 *Mustapha* [2007] EWCA Crim 1702, [38]. The Court quashed the conviction because the jury direction was inadequate, but upheld the co-defendant's conviction.

> *not subscribe to the view that it was necessary to re-litigate the whole matter, in our judgment it was inevitable that it had to be re-litigated. ... It was evidence of a single incident which ... only provided weak support for the identification of [D1]. Such probative value as it had was in our judgment overshadowed by its potential prejudicial effect. For these reasons, each member of this court would have excluded the evidence under s.101(3).*
>
> *"... we have concluded that the judge was wrong not to exclude the evidence. We add that, although the judge in his ruling made it perfectly clear that he was well aware of the need to consider s.101 (3) and s.78 of PACE in relation to the evidence, he gave no specific reasons for deciding that it should not be excluded under those provisions. It seems to us that judges should be careful in all such cases specifically to express their reasons for refusing an application to exclude such evidence. In our opinion, this is particularly important where the evidence relates to a previous acquittal."*[47]

A further problem with using acquittals is the application of s.109(1): is "*the evidence*" confined to the evidence of the allegation, or does it include the evidence of the acquittal as well? The CJA does not explicitly contemplate this point, but the answer might be implied from *Hussain*: any evidence of bad character that exists in relation to the acquittal consists only of the evidence of the allegation.[48]

By inference from *Z*, a jury can also go behind an agreed basis of plea to a conviction, where that conviction and the basis have been admitted as bad character evidence.[49]

Allegations that have been considered in a civil or tribunal context and resolved in favour of the subject of the allegations can still be admissible

47 *Mustapha* [2007] EWCA Crim 1702, [33]-[34].

48 *Hussain* [2008] EWCA Crim 1117.

49 *Wynes* [2014] EWCA Crim 2585, [15].

as bad character evidence in criminal proceedings.[50] It does not follow that the *conclusions* reached by the other court/tribunal are admissible.

2.2.2.2 The Fact Of The Acquittal Itself

Separately, and not necessarily as bad character, the actual fact of an acquittal can also be put before the jury. The Court of Appeal has described it as "*a very significant fact for the jury to consider*",[51] and has said "*[i]t would normally be relevant to consider the question of the admission of the fact of acquittal when considering admission of such evidence.*"[52]

However, contrast this statement in *Singh*: "*Evidence of a previous acquittal will generally be irrelevant and inadmissible because it is no more than evidence of the opinion of the jury in the previous trial.*"[53]

This does appear to be a very fact-specific decision. Caution should be exercised to avoid presenting the jury with a conundrum whereby they are asked to go into or behind the reasoning of a previous jury.

In *Singh*, the defendant faced trial on count 1 (murder of his second wife S) and count 2 (soliciting the murder of his first wife A some 5 years earlier). The first wife's relatives, including her brother B, gave evidence relating to count 2. The jury could not decide on count 1, and acquitted on count 2. At retrial on count 1, the defendant sought to suggest that B was responsible for S's death and had been hostile towards the defendant. In support of that contention, he wanted to cross-examine B to the effect that B had engineered false allegations and evidence in relation to count 2 which, by reason of the acquittal, had been disbelieved by the first jury.

---

50 *Hamidi* [2010] EWCA Crim 66, [26] onwards.

51 *Mustapha* [2007] EWCA Crim 1702, [39].

52 *Hajdarmataj* [2019] EWCA Crim 303, [46].

53 *Singh* [2022] EWCA Crim 1108, [42].

The Court of Appeal said,

(1) There may in a particular case be an exceptional feature which makes the evidence admissible, for example "*a situation in which a witness whose evidence at an earlier trial did not persuade the jury of that defendant's guilt is now giving evidence on a related matter in the second trial.*"

(2) However, in this case the acquittal at the first trial was not proof that the witnesses were lying in their evidence at that trial.

"*Indeed, we think that the circumstances in which an earlier acquittal can amount to such proof will be rare. Clearly the jury in the first trial were not satisfied that the prosecution had proved to the criminal standard all the requisite ingredients of the offence charged in Count 2; but the precise basis of their verdict is unknown, and no safe inference could be drawn that the jury must have found the [witnesses] to be liars.*"

(3) As evidence of the acquittal was inadmissible, the defence was also prohibited from relying upon the underlying material which would "*in our view, have served only to invite speculation by the jury*".

Similarly, in *McNeish*, evidence that the defendant had been acquitted of a more serious offence in a previous trial relating to the same incident was not considered admissible.[54]

54 *McNeish* [2015] EWCA Crim 2251. See also *Moore* [2023] EWCA Crim 1184 in relation to a co-defendant's acquittal.

2.2.2.3 *Police Cautions And Warnings*

Evidence underlying a police caution is evidence of bad character within the meaning of s.112(1).[55] Cautions are prime fuel for satellite litigation and should not be used routinely.

In *Pierce*, a caution admitted as bad character evidence was later "*deleted*" from the police record on application by D (primarily because D, having not seen the material on which the police had based their accusation, could not have made a clear and reliable admission). Since the true bad character evidence was the underlying evidence giving rise to the caution (including D's admissions in interview about that evidence), and not the caution itself, the later deletion of the caution did not threaten the safety of the conviction.[56]

Penalty notices and harassment warnings are not evidence of bad character.[57] They do not "*involve an admission of culpability. It follows that, at least ordinarily, we would not see a harassment warning of itself as capable of constituting bad character evidence*". However, when what is relied upon is the "*underlying material*" rather than the *warning* itself, it may, "*depending on the facts and circumstances*", be capable of constituting bad character evidence. Naturally, this then opens up risks of satellite litigation.

A penalty notice for disorder does not imply an admission of culpability and is not bad character evidence.[58] A person accepting such a notice would not believe that he was admitting guilt in respect of any offence.

---

55 *S* [2006] EWCA Crim 756, [2006] 2 Cr App R 23.

56 *Pierce* [2020] EWCA Crim 855, [35]-[36].

57 *Dalby* [2012] EWCA Crim 701, [22]. The complaint which formed the bad character evidence was also given by an anonymous witness, but as the defendant knew who she was, this was no reason not to allow the evidence.

58 *Hamer* [2010] EWCA Crim 2053, [2011] 1 Cr App R 3.

In *Hamer*, therefore, the judge was correct to give the defendant a good character direction, but the penalty notice was not relevant at all and should not have been admitted in the first place. Since it had been admitted, the judge should have explained the characteristics of a penalty notice.[59]

A warning letter from the Environment Agency referring to a "*suspected offence*" by a company of which the defendant was sole director, "*does not itself constitute any finding or admission of guilt and could not therefore impugn [D's] character*".[60]

2.3 "A Disposition Towards Misconduct"

Section 98 includes the following phrase: "*References in this Chapter to evidence of a person's 'bad character' are to evidence of, or of a disposition towards, misconduct on his part*".

"*Evidence of misconduct*" has been addressed above.

What is "*evidence of* a disposition towards *misconduct*"?

The legislation does not deal with the relationship between "*propensity*"[61] and "*disposition*". Nowhere in the Act is it explained what "*propensity*" or "*disposition*" mean, and it would not be wrong for someone familiar with the English language to accord a similar meaning to each word. Those

59 However, the conviction was still safe in the circumstances of the case.

60 *Mustafa v The Environment Agency* [2020] EWCA Crim 597, [86].

61 It is a named "*matter in issue*" (s.103(1)(a) and (b)) in respect of gateway (d); s.104(1) and usage indicate it is a commonly employed argument for gateway (e) as well.

familiar with statutory interpretation, however, would expect to find a different meaning for each word.[62]

It is unclear what the phrase "*evidence of a disposition towards misconduct*" adds to the concept of propensity.

The courts obviously consider "*propensity*" and "*disposition*" to be different, but perhaps only because they appear in different places in the Act. That is, a negative finding on s.103(1) (and thus on propensity in the two instances there) does not preclude other uses of the bad character evidence in question (which therefore still satisfies "*disposition*").

For a discussion of the meaning of "*propensity*", see Chapter 4 on gateway (d).

2.4 Evidence That Falls Within S.98(a)

> *"98 'Bad character'*
>
> *References in this Chapter [referring to Pt 11 Ch 1 of the CJA] to evidence of a person's 'bad character' are to evidence of, or of a disposition towards, misconduct on his part, other than evidence which—*
>
> *(a) has to do with the alleged facts of the offence with which the defendant is charged, or*
>
> *(b) is evidence of misconduct in connection with the investigation or prosecution of that offence.*

62 If propensity and disposition were intended to have the same meaning, then by virtue of s.98 all disposition bad character evidence already has the requisite propensity to satisfy s.103(1)(a) (in so far as a propensity towards misconduct is includes a propensity to commit offences of this kind). This would make the provision ineffectual.

"99 Abolition of common law rules

(1) The common law rules governing the admissibility of evidence of bad character in criminal proceedings are abolished.

(2) Subsection (1) is subject to section 118(1) in so far as it preserves the rule under which in criminal proceedings a person's reputation is admissible for the purposes of proving his bad character."

2.4.1 What Law Applies To Evidence Under S.98(a)?

Evidence that comes within s.98(a) (and s.98(b)) is not therefore automatically admissible.

The Court held in *Apabhai* that s.99 does not abolish the common law in respect of evidence that falls within s.98(a) and (b). Thus, "*if the evidence relied on falls within either section 98(a) or (b) then the common law rules are not abolished and continue to operate.*"[63]

A "*sufficient working model*" is to say that s.98(a) either:

> (1) encompasses "*evidence relating to the alleged facts of an offence which would have been admissible under the common law outside the context of bad character or propensity*"; or alternatively
>
> (2) encompasses anything "*directly relevant to the offence charged, provided … [it is] reasonably contemporaneous with and closely associated with its alleged facts*".[64]

Importantly, s.98(a) evidence can still be a trigger for gateway (g). See Chapter 4.

---

63 *Apabhai* [2011] EWCA Crim 917, [26]. See also *Edwards and Rowlands* [2005] EWCA Crim 3244, [2006] 2 Cr App R 4, [1]; *Watson* [2006] EWCA Crim 2308, [19]; *Fox* [2009] EWCA Crim 653, [27].

64 *McNeill* [2007] EWCA Crim 2927, [14].

Section 98(a) evidence can still be excluded under s.78 of PACE (see Chapter 5).

2.4.2 *"Has To Do With"*

This has been interpreted both broadly[65] and narrowly,[66] with recent case law tending towards the latter. While it is tempting to begin with a simple view (the words "*has to do with*" are "*ordinary English words*"[67]) the reality is that there is a wide grey area at the boundaries of these words ("*[t]he wording of section 98(a) is notoriously difficult to understand*"[68]). That was recognised recently in *Grundell*,[69] which approved the construction of s.98 given in *Mullings*.

The Court applied the temporal nexus test strictly in *Mullings*. For a fuller discussion of this case see Chapter 4 gateway (d) on gang-association. In the s.98(a) context, the Court held that letters received by the defendant several months after the offence, which contained information relevant to the gangs involved, was not evidence "*to do with*" the facts of the offence. While s.98(a) is not confined to the actus reus of the offence, the evidence failed the test of temporal connection or nexus. It was merely evidence of a general disposition.[70] A similar conclusion was reached in *McGowan*, where evidence of knives found at the defendant's home, and internet searches on his phone relating to knives, did not have

---

65 E.g. *Sule* [2012] EWCA Crim 1130, [2013] 1 Cr App R 3.

66 E.g. *McNeill* [2007] EWCA Crim 2927.

67 *Machado* [2006] EWCA Crim 837, [13]; *Lunkulu* [2015] EWCA Crim 1350, [23].

68 *Lewis* [2008] EWCA Crim 424, [13].

69 *Grundell* [2024] EWCA Crim 364, [43]. There, evidence of a non-sexual assault by D on C which allegedly took place some 14 hours following D's rape of C was not s.98(a) evidence, but was admissible via gateway (d).

70 *Mullings* [2010] EWCA Crim 2820, [2011] 2 Cr App R 2, [29]-[31].

the requisite nexus to the crime alleged. They were more properly gateway (d) propensity evidence.[71]

Guidance from the case law can be summarised as follows.

2.4.2.1 Temporal Nexus Usually Required

There is a strong temporal element in most cases.[72]

Evidence that is "*contemporaneous to and closely associated with the alleged facts of the offence*" falls within s.98(a).[73]

This is consistent with the original drafting of the legislation. The Law Commission intended the words in what later became s.98(a) to refer to a type of bad character evidence that would be admissible without the need for leave. It referred to such evidence as "*res gestae*": "*so inextricably linked to the facts about the offence charged, by reason of its close connection with them in time and space, that it should be automatically admissible*".[74]

In *Brummit*, the defendant was convicted of causing death by dangerous driving. Section 98(a) evidence included the fact that, twenty minutes prior to the incident, he had had an argument and scuffle with a shop owner, following which the defendant drove away, stopped and had a physical argument with another driver, and then drove away again very

---

71 *McGowan* [2023] EWCA Crim 247.

72 *Tirnaveanu* [2007] EWCA Crim 1239, [2007] 2 Cr App R 23. See also *Mullings* [2010] EWCA Crim 2820, [2011] 2 Cr App R 2; *McNeill* [2007] EWCA Crim 2927.

73 *Machado* [2006] EWCA Crim 837, [13].

74 *Evidence of Bad Character in Criminal Proceedings* (Law Com No 273, 2001), [10.3], see also [10.6].

quickly with the back doors open. "*[I]t was relevant to his state of mind and might shed some light on the manner of his driving thereafter.*"[75]

Per *Tirnaveanu*, the application of s.98 (the whole section) is a fact-specific exercise involving the interpretation of ordinary words. The exclusion in s.98(a) needed to "*be related to evidence where there is some* nexus in time *between the offence ... charged and the evidence of misconduct which the prosecution seek to adduce*".[76] Such a nexus did not exist on the facts in that case, as the prosecution was trying to adduce evidence of misconduct on a number of other occasions.

Tirnaveanu does not set limits for the required nexus or reveal the period of time under examination on the facts. However, it seems obvious that evidence relating to completely separate events, as in that case, could not fall within s.98(a).

Sule suggests the temporal requirement does not apply when the evidence in question is being "*relied upon as showing a motive for the index offence*".[77] This is because "*[t]he words of the statute are straightforward*" and do not include any temporal qualification.[78]

The *Sule* qualification should be confined to matters that reasonably show the genesis of the current charge; care should be taken to avoid

---

75 *Brummit* [2006] EWCA Crim 1629, [8]-[9]; similarly *Bishop* [2013] EWCA Crim 2413. See also *Spittle* [2008] EWCA Crim 2537 (as far as that case concerns past convictions that form elements of the present charges, such as breaching an ASBO or driving while disqualified); *DPP v Agyemang* [2009] EWHC 1542 (Admin).

76 *Tirnaveanu* [2007] EWCA Crim 1239, [2007] 2 Cr App R 23, [23] (emphasis added). See also *Sullivan* [2015] EWCA Crim 1565 (conviction unsafe).

77 *Sule* [2012] EWCA Crim 1130, [2013] 1 Cr App R 3, [11].

78 *Sule* [2012] EWCA Crim 1130, [2013] 1 Cr App R 3, [12]. *Stanton* [2021] EWCA Crim 1075, [34].

straying into areas of disputed motive, or disputed evidence of preparatory acts, that are more properly separate events.

Wrongful admission of such material can lead to satellite litigation. In *Milne*, the prosecution sought to establish motive for arson by showing that the complainant had owed the defendants a drugs debt. In support of that motive, the prosecution relied upon evidence that D1 was a drug dealer and D2 was a debt collector. The judge should not have admitted (under s.98(a) or any gateway) evidence of an alleged assault on a different person 6 months later showing a forensic connection to D2. As the judge told the jury:

> "*There's nothing to link this assault directly with D1. There's nothing to link this assault with any drug debt that might have been being enforced on D1's behalf. It is just one assault in January 2019, some months after the fire. It is an example of violent behaviour. That is all.*"

The Court of Appeal held that although the prosecution had been permitted to adduce evidence of motive, this did not make an example of violent behaviour by D2, 6 months after the fire, relevant.

> "*No application had been made to adduce evidence showing a general propensity to violence, unconnected with debt collecting or enforcement, and no such application could have succeeded. … the mere fact that he had been assaulted was of no relevance to the case against either [D], and it could therefore have no probative value. It was merely prejudicial evidence of violent behaviour by [D2].*"[79]

In *MA*, evidence of "*controlling and abusive behaviour*" in a relationship was partially admissible under s.98(a), but not those aspects of it that

[79] *Milne* [2022] EWCA Crim 753, [26]-[27].

were distanced in time or "*wholly unconnected to any particular piece of aggression*".[80] The latter were admissible under gateways (c) and (d).

There are, however, contrary examples.

In *Griggs*, evidence was admitted under s.98(a) of the defendant's sexual relationship with a 15-year-old girl (of necessity a criminal offence, and potentially of significant prejudicial effect) as going to a motive for killing his wife and to his own credibility. In the alternative, it was also gateway (c) and gateway (d) evidence.[81] This analysis appears to blur the careful (if complex) distinctions between each of these three avenues.

In *Alison*, keyword searches found on the defendant's devices were s.98(a) evidence in respect of allegations of making indecent photographs of children. That was so even where some of the search terms were older than the images in the charges.[82]

In *Malone*, the defendant was charged with murdering his wife. Police found in his house a document that he later admitted he had forged. It was a faked report, dated five months earlier, purporting to be from a private investigator whom the defendant had (genuinely) employed to follow his wife.[83] The forged document was s.98(a) evidence because it showed "*evidence of matrimonial difficulties, the intensity of the effect of these difficulties on the appellant and how he dealt with them before she disappeared*". This was

> "*admissible as evidence going directly to show with other circumstantial evidence that he had committed the offence. As such it was capable of being evidence 'to do with the alleged facts of the case' in the*

80 *MA* [2019] EWCA Crim 178, [39]-[41].

81 *Griggs* [2022] EWCA Crim 1115.

82 *Alison* [2021] EWCA Crim 324, [16].

83 *Malone* [2006] EWCA Crim 1860, [35].

> *same way as evidence to show a conspiracy or a joint venture would be admissible under section [98(a)].*"[84]

It might be argued that the connection is not so clear. In fact, the Court's final conclusion in *Malone* was that although the judge purported to use s.98(a), the evidence was eventually used in a propensity fashion instead. Thus, gateway (d) and s.103(1)(b) would have been satisfied because there was a question whether, after the wife's disappearance, the defendant was seen to lay a false trail as to what had happened to her. "*The issue was whether in relation to that conduct he was telling the truth.*"[85] This is more like gateway (d) evidence than s.98(a) evidence.

2.4.2.2 Elements Of The Offence Can Limit The Scope Of S.98(a)

In *Fox*, the defendant was accused of causing a child under 13 to engage in sexual activity by causing her to pose in indecent ways for photographs. The prosecution sought to prove bad character (an interest in pre-pubescent girls) via unproved allegations (the defendant's notebook and van, his behaviour towards three older girls whom he had photographed).

The Court held that the evidence was not "*to do with the alleged facts of the offence*". If it was, it would "*eliminate from the bad character provisions a great deal of evidence relating to propensity or motive. The reference in s.98(a) to the facts of the offence [is] to the actus reus. [In the present case] we are concerned with the applicant's intention and whether it was sexual—the*

84 *Malone* [2006] EWCA Crim 1860, [48].

85 *Malone* [2006] EWCA Crim 1860, [50]. The words 'important matter' are not used.

mens rea."[86] However, s.98(a) is not *confined* to the actus reus of the offence.[87]

In *Singh* it was said that the required nexus can be established "*on the basis that the evidence concerned directly relates to the defendant's motive or reasoning for committing the offence charged.*"[88] In that case, the evidence related to the alleged fabrication (by persons connected to the present offence) of evidence purporting to show that D had committed a different (but equally serious) crime some 5 years previously. D had been acquitted of that crime. The Court of Appeal held that this was not evidence that fell within s.98(a) or (b): "*Far from relating directly to the offence with which the appellant was charged therefore, it related to what was said by the appellant to be a false allegation by others of an offence which he had not committed and with which he was no longer charged.*"[89]

2.4.2.3 Limited By The Wording In The Gateways

"*The restrictions imposed by s.100 and 101 will be eroded, and their purpose impeded, if too wide an interpretation is given to paragraphs (a) and (b) of s.98*".[90]

Section 98(a) should be interpreted so as to direct evidence into the gateways, so that more evidence falls within the statutory remit than within the common law.[91]

---

86 *Fox* [2009] EWCA Crim 653, [25].

87 *Mullings* [2010] EWCA Crim 2820, [2011] 2 Cr App R 2, [29]. See also *IA* [2013] EWCA Crim 1308, [114].

88 *Singh* [2022] EWCA Crim 1108, [37].

89 *Singh* [2022] EWCA Crim 1108, [38].

90 *Singh* [2022] EWCA Crim 1108, [37].

91 *McNeill* [2007] EWCA Crim 2927; see also *Edwards and Rowlands* [2005] EWCA Crim 3244, [2006] 2 Cr App R 4; *Wallace* [2007] EWCA Crim

From the point of view of the subject of the bad character evidence, it may be more desirable that the evidence falls within the statute, as then the procedure in s.100 or s.101 must be followed.

Section 98(a) generally provides an easier route to admissibility than the gateways. Therefore, the Court has taken the view that if a gateway is satisfied, it is unnecessary to consider whether s.98(a) was the correct avenue on the facts.[92]

In *Rowe*, the defendant G in cross-examination denied knowing members of two rival gangs and denied knowledge of firearms. The Court of Appeal said that evidence contradicting this was actually s.98(a) evidence, but in any event it was plainly admissible via gateway (f).[93]

The main confusion occurs in the overlap between s.98(a) and gateway (c): see below.[94]

1760, [2008] 1 WLR 572. In *Vehicle and Operator Services Agency v Ace Crane and Transport Ltd* [2010] EWHC 288 (Admin), previous uncharged breaches of transport regulations were "*to do with*" the present charge for breaching the same regulations. *Mullings* [2010] EWCA Crim 2820, [2011] 2 Cr App R 2, [32] attempts to narrow s.98(a) by requiring temporal nexus; see also *Saleem* [2007] EWCA Crim 1923; *Scott* [2009] EWCA Crim 2457.

92 *Swellings* [2009] EWCA Crim 3249, [2009] 2 Cr App R (S) 30, [52].

93 *Rowe* [2022] EWCA Crim 27, [90]-[91].

94 There is occasional overlap between s.98(a) and gateway (d); the other gateways tend to have less. See *Lovelock* [2007] EWCA Crim 476 (s.98(a) and not (f)); *L* [2009] EWCA Crim 2688 (gateway (e) rather than s.98(a)); *Watson* [2006] EWCA Crim 2308 (s.98(a) instead of gateways (d) or (g)); *Ravjani* [2012] EWCA Crim 2519 (probably not admissible under either gateway (e) or s.98(a)).

2.4.2.4 Evidence Of Offences Committed By D At The Same Time

Evidence of offences committed by the defendant at the same time as the present offence can be s.98(a) evidence. Typically, this is confined to offences to which the defendant has pleaded guilty and which have some relevance to the defendant's guilt in respect of the current offence.

As a matter of good practice, prosecutors do not routinely seek to rely on guilty pleas to associated offences without something more.

For example, although the defendant's guilty plea to driving a car without insurance might technically be s.98(a) evidence in respect of his trial for possessing an offensive weapon in the boot of that car, it will not normally be helpful or fair to admit it purely on this basis.

This category can also include the defendant's conviction at trial for an offence committed at the same time as the present offence. For example, if the defendant is convicted of count 1 at trial 1, but the jury are hung on count 2, the conviction for count 1 can be admissible at the retrial for count 2. There will usually need to be some temporal or other connection between the counts; usually, this will be satisfied by the same reasons given for the counts appearing together on the indictment in the first place.[95]

In *Watson*[96] the defendant was convicted, on retrial, for the rape of his wife. At the first trial he was convicted of assault occasioning actual bodily harm against his wife arising from the same events, but the jury could not agree on the rape charge. The assault was said to have happened just before the rape and was connected with an argument the couple were having. At retrial on the rape, the evidence of the ABH conviction was admissible via s.98(a).

---

95 See, e.g., *Abdullah* [2019] EWCA Crim 1137.

96 *Watson* [2006] EWCA Crim 2308.

2.4.2.5 Evidence Of Offences Committed By A Co-Defendant

D2's guilty plea to an offence which arises out of the same facts as those which give rise to D1's current trial can be admissible via s.98(a). Caution should be exercised: it is vital not to prevent the jury from being able independently to decide D1's guilt. In *Horne*, admission of the co-defendant's plea to conspiracy "*would have tended significantly to close down the central issue relevant to this count*".[97]

If D2 is now not taking part in the trial at all, s.98(a) or s.100 (*not* s.101) applies (see Chapter 3).

If D2 remains a party to the trial, s.98(a) or s.101 applies (see Chapter 4).

Section 78 of PACE may operate to exclude D2's guilty plea (see Chapter 5).

Bear in mind that D2's offence must arise out of the same facts. Thus, D2's plea to a burglary would be s.98(a) evidence if D1 was charged with the same burglary. But if D1 is charged instead with handling stolen goods from that burglary, D2's plea to committing that burglary will not necessarily be s.98(a) evidence. This is due to the temporal limitations mentioned above.

An exception to this might arise from *Olive*. There, D1's knowledge of her son, D2's, previous convictions for violence "*could properly form part of the basis for deciding whether, if the jury accepted that [D1] drove [D2] to the scene of the crime, [D1] did so knowing what [D2] was intending to do there.*"[98]

---

97 *Horne* [2020] EWCA Crim 487.

98 *Olive* [2022] EWCA Crim 1141, [86].

2.4.3 Section 98(a), Gateway (c) and Res Gestae

It can be difficult to distinguish between evidence that has to do with the offence (s.98(a)) and evidence that completes another, otherwise inexplicable, piece of evidence (gateway (c)).

Early on, the Court of Appeal indicated that there would be problems caused by the overlap between s.98(a) and gateway (c): "*difficult questions can arise as to whether evidence of background or motive falls to be admitted under those exclusions in s.98 or requires consideration under s.101(1)(c).*"[99]

The Court of Appeal has concluded that it does not matter whether s.98(a) or gateway (c) allows the use of the evidence in question, as they have no practical dissimilarity: *"In practice nothing of any legal significance depends on which of these two routes it is by which the evidence comes in."*[100]

It is, nonetheless, good practice both in terms of fairness and appeal considerations, to ascertain the correct avenue so that the appropriate exclusionary provisions are applied and the jury can be properly directed on the use of the evidence.[101]

Note that s.98(a) and gateway (c) are only similar (if at all), when the evidence is actually capable of being admitted via both. In any other situation, their differences matter greatly. For example, and very obviously, if the evidence does *not* fall within s.98(a), then gateway (c) needs to be examined properly. To say that one will satisfy the situation if the other

99 *Edwards and Rowlands* [2005] EWCA Crim 3244, [2006] 2 Cr App R 4, [1](i).

100 *Tirnaveanu* [2007] EWCA Crim 1239, [2007] 2 Cr App R 23, [24], agreeing with Professor Spencer. See also *Henderson* [2010] EWCA Crim 1269, [2010] 2 Cr App R 24; *Haigh* [2010] EWCA Crim 90; *Rossi* [2009] EWCA Crim 2406.

101 *AG* [2018] EWCA Crim 1393, [31]-[32]. Contrast the approach in *Mufty* [2017] EWCA Crim 185, [19]-[20], where neither the definition of bad character, s.98(a), nor any gateways were considered.

does not, is to risk ignoring the conditions that come with each.[102] It may be appropriate to say, as in *McPherson*: "*In this case we have no doubt that the evidence of the [bad character] was, in principle, admissible. Either it is evidence which is connected with the facts of the offence, or it is evidence of criminal behaviour falling within the statutory definition of bad character.*"[103] But merely being evidence of bad character within the statute does not mean that the necessary legislative conditions under a particular gateway are satisfied. The next step is to examine those conditions.

Gateway (c) certainly comes with extra requirements, notably of substantial value and the impossibility or difficulty of understanding the other evidence. The breadth of s.98(a) is actually *limited* by the context provided by the gateways, notably by gateway (c):

> *"'has to do with' are words of prima facie broad application, albeit constituting a phrase that has to be construed in the overall context of the bad character provisions of the 2003 Act. Thus the breadth of the words are clearly limited by the context for instance of section 101(1)(c)'s reference to important explanatory evidence, and gateway (d)'s more general reference to important matter in issue, which taken together with section 103 relates to propensity and previous convictions."*[104]

A further complication is whether the common law of res gestae has survived s.98(a) and gateway (c), and to what extent. This necessitates an examination of the Law Commission's proposals and how they were adopted into the CJA.

---

102 E.g. s.102 in *Martin* [2005] EWCA Crim 3259.

103 *McPherson* [2010] EWCA Crim 2906, [17].

104 *McNeill* [2007] EWCA Crim 2927, [14].

The original drafting made the following distinction:[105]

- What became s.98(a) was drafted to cover evidence "*so inextricably linked to the facts about the offence charged, by reason of its close connection with them in time and space, that it should be automatically admissible*". The Law Commission intended this to refer to a type of bad character evidence that would be admissible without the need for leave. It referred to such evidence as "*res gestae*".

- A distinction was made with other evidence which, "*though not forming part of the alleged facts, is nonetheless linked to those central facts by virtue of its force in making them comprehensible.*" Such evidence, contributing to comprehension rather than merely being inextricable, later became the subject of gateway (c) and s.100(1)(a) and *did* require a test of admissibility.

In the draft Bill, only the first type of evidence was to be considered true res gestae evidence and worthy of admission without leave.[106] But both types of evidence are still bad character evidence as defined by the CJA. As a result, the common law pertaining to both types of evidence was abolished by s.99. This would mean that the common law on res gestae as it mirrors the words of 98(a) is abolished.

2.5 Section 98(b)

By contrast to s.98(a), s.98(b) is relatively straightforward and rarely used. It is designed to apply to misconduct that is related to, but not

---

[105] *Evidence of Bad Character in Criminal Proceedings* (Law Com No 273, 2001), [10.3], see also [10.6].

[106] *Evidence of Bad Character in Criminal Proceedings* (Law Com No 273, 2001), [10.3]. It may be that such evidence (for which leave was not required) was considered to be so strong as to justify its inclusion without passing further tests.

actually part of, the offending charged. It is not confined to misconduct committed by someone acting for the prosecuting authority. It can be committed by any person, including a defendant or defence witness, or someone who does not in fact give evidence at all.

Thus, in *Apabhai*, an allegation that D2 had blackmailed D1 for money in exchange for not incriminating D1 in the upcoming trial, was admissible at D1's behest under s.98(b).

> *"The fact that the evidence demonstrates bad character is not the central feature justifying its admission. Its principal purpose is to demonstrate a motive for D2 putting the appellant in the frame, and the fact that the evidence also demonstrates bad character is incidental. For example, there may be a case where a co-defendant is alleged to bear a grudge because of some slight, real or imagined, from the defendant and this is said to explain why he is lying about the defendant. Such evidence would surely be admissible even though it does not disclose bad character by the co-defendant."*[107]

For an example of a situation that occurred during trial, which was not s.98(b) evidence and not admissible, see *Mahil.*[108]

Section 98(b) does not include other offences with which the defendant is charged that have arisen out of the same facts, regardless of whether the defendant pleads guilty to those other offences or not.[109] Note that two or more offences against the same defendant are to be treated as separate offences in separate proceedings (see s.112(2)). Section 98(b) therefore does not include, for example, an offence (offence 2) of assaulting a police

[107] *Apabhai* [2011] EWCA Crim 917, [33]. See also *Haxhiaj* [2016] EWCA Crim 83 regarding threats to the defendant made before trial, but cf Crutchley [2021] EWCA Crim 1001 concerning threats made by a co-defendant during trial.

[108] *Mahil* [2013] EWCA Crim 673.

[109] *Edwards* [2005] EWCA Crim 1813, [2006] 1 Cr App R 3, [43].

officer while being arrested for offence 1. If the defendant pleads guilty to offence 2, evidence of that offence is not admissible via s.98(b) in a trial for offence 1. It may be admissible via s.98(a), or a s.101 gateway (subject to exclusionary provisions).

2.6 Procedure: Notice/Application/Objections

A party applies to admit bad character evidence under s.100.

A party gives notice of the intent to use bad character evidence under s.101. No *application* is needed under s.101 (unlike s.100). A party only needs to give notice (within a prescribed time period, and via s.111 and the Criminal Procedure Rules Part 21) of its intent to use bad character evidence under one of the s.101 gateways.

However, practitioners and courts overwhelmingly use the terminology of 'application' rather than that of 'notice', perhaps reflecting that the final decision on admissibility is for the judge to make. Nothing in practice turns upon the difference.

In principle, a judge can suggest that the prosecution serve a bad character application/notice, "*provided that a judge is scrupulous in not taking on the function of the prosecutor or appearing to do so. Any such suggestion to the prosecution should be carefully expressed, not least because the judge may not be aware of what has been agreed between the trial advocates.*"[110] There would appear to be no reason why a judge cannot make a similar suggestion to the defence.

Under s.110 and r.21.5, a court is required to give reasons in open court when it makes a decision on any of s.98 (whether something is evidence of bad character), s.100, s.101, s.101(3), or s.107.

---

110 *Omotoso* [2018] EWCA Crim 1394, [47].

Parties are encouraged to apply/give notice with due care and detail, and judges to identify the applicable gateways and exclusions in a ruling.[111]

2.6.1 Time limits

The judge has a discretion in respect of the time limits and should exercise it.[112] The fact that there is technically no power to 'refuse leave' may underlie the courts' readiness to dispense with the time period for prosecution notice. That is, courts are more prepared to exercise their discretion not to exclude because they realise that the tenor of the Act (evidenced in part by the mere 'notice' terminology) is to give more weight to the prosecution's decision to use the evidence.

For an example of an "*unacceptable delay*", see *Urushadze*, where the prosecution indicated at the start of an adjourned retrial that it would be giving notice, and then gave the actual notice orally, with details of the previous convictions, very close to the end of the prosecution case.[113] The appeal was allowed because the evidence should not have been admitted, regardless of the delay.

The precise time limits and requirements are currently set out in the Crim PR at rules 21.2, 21.3 and 21.4. In practice, following the forms produced on the justice.gov.uk website will ensure compliance. Key points to note are:

---

111 *PB* [2016] EWCA Crim 1462, [43]: "*Had the proper procedures been followed it is likely that the confusion that has led to this appeal would not have arisen. Further, as bad character evidence, even without a written application the judge should have identified the applicable gateway(s) of admissibility and addressed section 101(3) of the Criminal Justice Act 2003 in his ruling.*"

112 See, e.g., *Bovell and Dowds* [2005] EWCA Crim 1091, [2005] 2 Cr App R 27, [2].

113 *Urushadze* [2008] EWCA Crim 2498, [19].

- The prosecutor generally has a time limit of 10 business days after a not guilty plea to serve an application or notice (in the magistrates' court for prosecutors it is 20 days in respect of a s.101 notice);

- Other parties generally must serve an application or notice within 10 business days;

- Any objection from any party must be served within 10 business days;

- Applications/notices/objections should contain at least a summary of the substantive argument being made;

- A defendant who wants to use gateway (b) (introduce evidence of his own bad character) must at the latest give notice of this prior to the evidence being introduced (r.21.4(8)). While there is no mechanism to object or exclude this evidence (save perhaps a baseline rule of relevance to the trial), gateway (b) is not a 'surprise' gateway.

2.6.2 When Should the Admissibility of Bad Character Evidence Be Determined?

This is a case-specific exercise. It depends on the gateway(s) being used and the nature and availability of the evidence. The Court of Appeal has generally refused to set down any specific schedule.[114] It may be desirable to determine any obvious bad character matters early on in the trial process in order to avoid problems of the sort that arose in *Joyce* (a case decided under the Northern Ireland equivalent):

> "*There is good reason for a judge to make his ruling on the admissibility of bad character at the start of the case. … We are of the view*

[114] *D* [2006] EWCA Crim 1703.

> *that in the present case the application to adduce bad character evidence should have taken place at the start of the trial to have allowed the appellant to know precisely what he faced at an early stage, prepare and manage his defence and adapt his cross-examination accordingly.*"[115]

In *Lewis*, the judge should have determined admissibility of the defendant's previous convictions *before* considering whether to order disclosure surrounding the circumstances in which some of the convictions had occurred. That was important because the defendant contended that he had been a police informant when he had pleaded guilty to certain offences. Disclosure of material surrounding this contention led to complications and delays, which may have been avoided had the bad character issue been ruled on first.[116]

2.7 Section 74 Of PACE

Section 74 of PACE is not an avenue for *admitting* evidence. It is often erroneously cited as such. Its function is now confined to the provability (presentation and proof) of evidence that has *already been admitted.*

As originally enacted, s.74(1) was a test of admissibility:

> "*(1) In any proceedings the fact that a person other than the accused has been convicted of an offence by or before any court in the United Kingdom or by a Service court outside the United Kingdom shall be admissible in evidence for the purpose of proving, where to do so is relevant to any issue in those proceedings, that that person committed that offence, whether or not any other evidence of his having committed that offence is given.*" (old version)

115 *Joyce* [2023] NICA 67, [112]-[113].

116 *Lewis* [2022] EWCA Crim 237, [2024] 2 Cr App R 9, [62].

It was amended by the CJA[117] and now reads:

> "*(1) In any proceedings the fact that a person other than the accused has been convicted of an offence by or before any court in the United Kingdom or by a Service court outside the United Kingdom shall be admissible in evidence for the purpose of proving that that person committed that offence, where evidence of his having done so is admissible, whether or not any other evidence of his having committed that offence is given.*" (current version)

Sub-section 74(3) is a parallel provision in respect of the accused's convictions.

The phrase "*where to do so is relevant to any issue in those proceedings*" has been replaced with "*where evidence of his having done so is admissible*". Thus, admissibility is a prerequisite for the use of s.74.

Were this not the case, and convictions were rendered *admissible* by s.74, then we might be justified in questioning the purpose of s.100 and s.101 of the CJA. As it is, the legislative structure requires admissibility first (via the CJA), followed by the practical means of proving the details of the admissible evidence (via s.74). Section 74 is used to avoid the need for the jury to decide whether that offence was committed, but does not make evidence of the offence admissible.

Per the Court of Appeal in *Kordasinski* (in the context of foreign convictions, making the point that admissibility is different from provability):

> "*It is, as we have said, necessary to distinguish between admissibility and how admissible evidence may be proved. In our judgment, the Polish convictions were admissible pursuant to and subject to s.101(1)(d) and (g), and s.103 of the 2003 Act. The rule*

[117] By the Criminal Justice Act 2003 Sch.36(5) para.85(2), having effect from 15 December 2004; further amended by (EU Exit) Regulations on 31 December 2020.

> *in* Hollington v Hewthorn *was abolished for criminal cases, in so far as it may ever have applied or have survived, by s.99(1) of the 2003 Act. The convictions were provable, as opposed to admissible, under s.7 of the 1851 Act, whose formalities were complied with in this case."*[118]

It is likely that *Moore*, where s.74 was cited as the avenue for admitting convictions of persons described as "co-defendants" tried during the first of two separate trials, should also have made mention of the Criminal Justice Act 2003.[119]

Despite s.74, a defendant is entitled to seek to demonstrate that he did not in fact commit the offence that is proved via s.74(3).[120] He bears the burden of proof (balance of probabilities) in this regard and may be able to call fresh evidence in support. He is not, however, entitled to turn the current trial into a retrial of the earlier offences simply by recalling the same evidence from the earlier trial.[121]

2.8 Relevance

> *"Judges must have in mind that no evidence is admissible unless it is relevant to the issues in the case and there is a duty to consider in advance all evidence that the parties propose to place before the jury."*[122]

---

118 *Kordasinski* [2006] EWCA Crim 2984, [2007] 1 Cr App R 17, [72]-[73].

119 *Moore* [2023] EWCA Crim 1184.

120 *C* [2010] EWCA Crim 2971, [2011] 1 WLR 1942, *Tarik Hill* [2021] EWCA Crim 587, *Caine* [2024] EWCA Crim 225.

121 *Obi* [2024] EWCA Crim 805.

122 Crown Court Compendium Part I: Jury and Trial Management and Summing Up, 12.1(2). References are to the July 2024 version. See also the

This fundamental rule applies to all bad character evidence, regardless of whether other conditions in the CJA are satisfied.

The concept of relevance also appears in several places within the CJA provisions on bad character.

2.8.1 Definition Of 'Relevance'

Stephens' definition of 'relevant' from the *Digest of the Law of Evidence* is most often cited as the legal standard of relevance:

> *"any two facts to which ['relevant'] is applied are so related to each other that according to the common course of events one either taken by itself or in connection with other facts proves or renders probable the past, present, or future existence or non-existence of the other."*[123]

This may be summarised, for convenience, as whether fact *x* proves or renders probable or improbable fact *y*.

The Law Commission has said that "*[r]elevant, in this context, means having some probative value on a matter in issue in the proceedings.*"[124] There is, however, no definitive meaning of either 'relevance' or 'probative value'.

In addition to its threshold function as the keystone to admissibility of all evidence, the additional presence of relevance in gateways (d), (e) and (f) performs two further functions:

---

leading case of *Hanson* [2005] EWCA Crim 824, [2005] 2 Cr App R 21, [27].

123 Fitzjames Stephen's *Digest of the Law of Evidence* (12th edn, Macmillan 1948) art 1.

124 *Evidence of Bad Character in Criminal Proceedings* (Law Com No 273, 2001), [5.7].

1) To direct our attention to the 'feature' of the case to which the evidence must be relevant.

    a. In the case of gateways (d) and (e), that feature is an important matter in issue between the appropriate parties.

    b. In gateway (f), the feature is the correction of a false impression—as indicated by the requirement of probative value in s.105(1)(b).

2) To establish the standard of relevance required.

    a. For gateways (d) and (f) it is simply probative value.

    b. For gateway (e), this is substantial probative value rather than just probative value (or mere relevance). "*Substantial probative value*" must mean something more than "*relevant*" and "*probative value*" in (d) and (f).[125]

While gateway (e) (and s.100(1)(b), which uses the same threshold) is perhaps looking for a logical link, the simplified wording in gateways (d) and (f) suggests the lower standard of bare relevance, rejecting any enhanced standard for admission (and, for (d), leaving prejudice to be dealt with by s.101(3) and s.103(3)).[126]

Gateways (a), (b), (c) and (g) do not contain any repeated requirement of relevance. Gateways (a) and (b) do not need it, because the feature to which the evidence is relevant will usually be accepted by the defendant,[127] and with his agreement there is no need for further safeguards of enhanced relevance. Gateway (c) implicitly requires relevance to the

125 See Chapter 5 gateway (e).

126 As in *Woodhead* [2011] EWCA Crim 472, [23]-[24] (in the context of gateway (g)).

127 Subject to the *Highton* principle: see Chapter 4 gateway (g).

thing that is being explained. Gateway (g) lacks a feature to which bad character evidence has to be relevant.

In summary, therefore, relevance performs the vital function of telling us how probative evidence *x* must be to feature *y* (where the evidence is the bad character evidence, and the feature is the thing to which the evidence must be directed).

2.8.2 Section 109 Assumption Of Truth

"109 Assumption of truth in assessment of relevance or probative value

(1) Subject to subsection (2), a reference in this Chapter to the relevance or probative value of evidence is a reference to its relevance or probative value on the assumption that it is true.

(2) In assessing the relevance or probative value of an item of evidence for any purpose of this Chapter, a court need not assume that the evidence is true if it appears, on the basis of any material before the court (including any evidence it decides to hear on the matter), that no court or jury could reasonably find it to be true."

Section 112(1) states: "*'probative value', and 'relevant' (in relation to an item of evidence), are to be read in accordance with section 109"*.

Section 109 is designed to deal with the situation where the bad character is disputed. The tribunal of law (as opposed to the tribunal of fact) is required to assume that the alleged bad character evidence is true (the first stage) before proceeding to the question whether the evidence satisfies a gateway of admissibility (the second stage). Eliding the two stages can result in an erroneous ruling.[128] *Dizaei* sets out the difference:

> *"the assumption in s.109 is not determinative of the admissibility question. Rather it provides the context in which the admissibility*

[128] *Luckett* [2015] EWCA Crim 1050, [26]-[28].

> *decision falls to be made. In short, the pre-conditions to admissibility under [any gateway] are not automatically established, and, notwithstanding the evidential assumptions provided by s.109 at the admissibility stage, the bare fact of an allegation (even if assumed to be true) is not necessarily conclusive of the question whether it [passes the particular legislative test for admissibility]."*[129]

However, "*the evidential assumption in s.109 does not bind the jury, and the investigation of this evidence at trial may be liable to distract attention from the crucial issue which is whether the case against the defendant has been proved.*"[130] If the evidence is admitted, and not excluded, the jury will need to be directed as to how to treat the truth of the evidence (see Chapter 6).

Section 109 applies to <u>all</u> evidence (whether relied on by the prosecution or the defence) in respect of which an assessment of relevance or probative value is required under ss.98-113. It applies to evidence that is evidence of bad character, and thus, by implication, does not apply to evidence that falls *within* s.98(a) or s.98(b):

> *"Section 101(1) refers to evidence of a defendant's bad character and section 101(1)(e) refers to "it", namely bad character that is misconduct on the part of the appellant as defined in section 98. The reference in section 109(1) to an assumption that 'it' is true, is a reference back to bad character as defined by section 98".*[131]

The principle in s.109(2) has been described as creating a "*rebuttable*" assumption of truth.[132] There is little guidance on what would be sufficient material to justify a conclusion that no tribunal of fact could reasonably find the evidence to be true. In most cases, something that is so

---

129 *Dizaei* [2013] EWCA Crim 88, [2013] 1 Cr App R 31, [36].

130 *Dizaei* [2013] EWCA Crim 88, [2013] 1 Cr App R 31, [37].

131 *Mitchell* [2010] EWCA Crim 783, [17].

132 *Gabbana* [2020] EWCA Crim 1473, [44].

patently untrue as to satisfy s.109(2) is likely to be very obvious indeed. In *Musone*, the Court said:

> *"Section 109 gives rise to a stark choice between either an assumption that the evidence is true or rejection of its truth on the grounds that no court or jury could reasonably find it to be true. But in reality … there will be evidence which, although capable of belief, is improbable and unlikely to be believed."*[133]

In practice it does appear that s.109(1) is of less assistance to the defence than to the prosecution. In *Braim*, although s.109 was not specifically referenced, the Court of Appeal concluded that an allegation by person O about the deceased J was not admissible at D's trial for the murder of J, in part because O was unwilling to give evidence about that allegation and its probative value was therefore diminished.[134] Perhaps s.109(1) might have mitigated against this.

In *Portman* C had previously made a similar allegation of racially aggravated language against person B, which had resulted in B's acquittal.[135] The defendant wished to rely upon this (s.100(1)(b)) as evidence of what he said was a false complaint of a similar nature to the one he now faced. That application was refused because, "taking matters at their highest, all that could properly be inferred from the fact that the appeal was allowed was that the Court could not be sure that the words … were used".[136] The Court held that it did not follow that C had "positively lied". However, it might be argued that where C claimed he had heard B say

[133] *Musone* [2007] EWCA Crim 1237, [2007] 2 Cr App R 29, [60].

[134] *Braim* [2022] EWCA Crim 352, [38].

[135] Convicted by the magistrates, D appealed to the Crown Court which allowed the appeal. No formal transcript or record of the hearing was available but the judge heard evidence from the officer in the case on a voir dire to the effect that C had told him the conviction had been quashed because the Crown Court was not sure C could have heard the words alleged.

[136] *Portman* [2022] EWCA Crim 1200, [44].

something and a court found that he had not done so, that finding taken with s.109(1) was relevant to C's credibility (as someone who was mistaken, if not lying).

Of course, there is no way to exclude defence evidence that meets the test under s.100(1)(b), which might explain the stricter approach taken under s.109. Thus, an additional condition of "*fairness*" appears to have emerged in relation to evidence relied upon by the defence, because of the absence of the exclusionary provisions that can be applied at a later stage:

> *"cases in which a breach of the procedural rules will entitle a court to exclude evidence of substantial probative value will be rare. A court should be most reluctant to exclude evidence of that quality by reason of a breach of the procedural code. Nonetheless, there will be cases, of which the instant appeal is an example, where the only way in which the court can ensure fairness is by excluding evidence, even when it reaches the quality described in section 101(1)(e). ...* ***Whilst the judge is compelled to assume the truth of such evidence for the purposes of section 101(1)(e), he need not take so extreme a view when considering whether to prevent the unfair effect of a breach of the procedural rules by excluding the evidence.*** *The more credible the evidence, the less likely it is that the judge will exclude it on grounds of a breach of a procedural requirement. But where, as in the instant case, the evidence is improbable, the judge is entitled to take that factor into account in deciding whether to exclude it, in circumstances where the rules have been deliberately breached."*[137]

That pragmatic approach should be balanced against the need to avoid diminishing the assumption because the evidence comes from a non-prosecution source. Thus, in *Luckett*, the Court emphasised that "*[i]f the allegations were true—and the assumption is that they were true—then they*

---

137 *Musone* [2007] EWCA Crim 1237, [2007] 2 Cr App R 29, [60] (emphasis added).

clearly had substantial probative value in the context of this case. The fact that the allegation came from [D] alone was not, of itself, a reason for refusing the application."[138]

2.8.3 If Irrelevant, Do Not Admit

The Court of Appeal periodically issues this reminder.

In the gateway (d) case of *Bullen*, the defendant was convicted of murder, having pleaded guilty to manslaughter on the basis that his intoxication negated the element of specific intent. The only matter in issue was whether the defendant had intended to kill or cause grievous bodily harm.

The prosecution argument was that the defendant's previous convictions (mainly for violent behaviour, often involving guilty pleas), were relevant to a propensity to violence "*which therefore made it more likely than might otherwise have been the case that the defendant was guilty of murder*".[139]

The Court of Appeal disagreed. The prosecution had initially intended the bad character evidence to be used in relation to a plea of self-defence, but once the defendant pleaded to manslaughter, the use of the evidence was not "*rethought or adapted*".[140] As propensity to violence was no longer an issue, the evidence was not relevant. As the defendant had pleaded guilty to manslaughter, previous convictions "*of (relatively low level) violence*"[141] were not admissible to prove the specific intent required for murder.

---

138 *Luckett* [2015] EWCA Crim 1050, [27]. Compare *A* [2020] EWCA Crim 1687.

139 *Bullen* [2008] EWCA Crim 4, [2008] 2 Cr App R 25, [17].

140 *Bullen* [2008] EWCA Crim 4, [2008] 2 Cr App R 25, [27].

141 *Bullen* [2008] EWCA Crim 4, [2008] 2 Cr App R 25, [1].

In a particularly clear tribute to relevance, the Court of Appeal said that despite the changes made by the CJA to render bad character evidence more readily admissible, "*the test is still relevance*". Gateway (d) requires it, as does the introductory language of s.101. The fact that propensity is always a potential matter in issue owing to s.103(1) "*should not be overstated to the extent that sight is lost of the need for relevance: the bad character must still be relevant to an 'important' issue.*" And propensity will not be a matter in issue at all where the proviso to s.103(1)(a) operates.[142] The "*safeguard*" of s.103(3) itself "*emphasises the significance of relevance's handmaiden, probative value.*"[143]

The Court of Appeal was also critical of a "*lack of focus*" in the judge's treatment of the three *Hanson* questions.[144] He failed to take properly into account the limited nature of the issue at trial—limited by the defendant's plea to manslaughter. When considering if the convictions actually established a propensity under s.103(1)(a) (question one), the judge focused only on their violent aspect. "*He added that, save in one instance, the violence was 'deliberate' but that, in our judgment, was an unsatisfactory and potentially misleading gloss, if it was intended as such, on the concept of specific intent.*"[145] The Court said that "*a propensity to commit offences of the kind charged*" is a "*deliberately broad concept, properly designed for the generality of cases, but to be handled with care when the sole issue was specific intent.*" Question two of *Hanson* presented the "*only real opportunity*" to consider relevance, since the judge

142 *Bullen* [2008] EWCA Crim 4, [2008] 2 Cr App R 25, [30]-[31]: the Court refers to the Explanatory Notes to the CJA, and distinguishes *Duggan* (*Edwards* [2005] EWCA Crim 1813, [2006] 1 Cr App R 3) where the defendant claimed he was entirely innocent and pleaded self-defence and so a propensity to violence was relevant.

143 *Bullen* [2008] EWCA Crim 4, [2008] 2 Cr App R 25, [29].

144 See Chapter 4 gateway (d).

145 *Bullen* [2008] EWCA Crim 4, [2008] 2 Cr App R 25, [33].

> *"nowhere asked himself the question whether the appellant having the propensity in question is, or is relevant to, an 'important' matter in issue ... [he] answered that question merely by saying that it was open to the jury to conclude that it did, after receiving a proper direction. ... if it was to be 'Yes', the judge should have explained what light in particular the previous convictions were capable of throwing on the case with which he was concerned."*

Finally, the Court held that the judge was wrong to dismiss question three, for it seems unjust or unfair "*to rely on a raft of previous convictions which are not in themselves suggested to throw any light on the issue of intent before the jury.*"[146] This essentially restates the absence of relevance.

2.9 Good Character

Good character is, at its lowest, simply an absence of bad character.

This basic good character can be distinguished from what is sometimes called *positive* good character, namely evidence of behaviour that is perceived by society as actively desirable (as opposed to a mere lack of evidence of reprehensible behaviour). Typically, such moral or social good behaviour is shown through character references[147] or evidence of charitable, voluntary, community or other public service (including certain professions[148]).

Historically, the weight accorded to good character and the generosity of good character directions were partly designed to compensate for the defendant's handicaps at trial, especially the prohibition on testifying in his

---

[146] *Bullen* [2008] EWCA Crim 4, [2008] 2 Cr App R 25, [33].

[147] As to the value of these see *McChleery* [2019] EWCA Crim 2100, [19].

[148] E.g. religious employment, emergency services work, military service, etc.

own defence.[149] And, because he could not give evidence, a good character direction would not (as it now can) touch upon his credibility. Today, good character has assumed a different role. In effect, a defendant is entitled to it if he does not have a bad character.

Good character evidence is usually greatly diffused, existing at a high level of generality (focusing on the entirety of the defendant's behaviour over the course of many years), whereas bad character evidence usually appears in the form of particularised instances. This leads to the result that a specific point of bad character will rebut a general account of good character, but neither a general account nor a specific instance of good character will negate a specific point of bad character. The usefulness of good character evidence is not readily assessed in the same way as that of bad character evidence.

The standard good character direction is designed for basic good character. An enhanced direction can be given where positive good character has been relied on. The essence of the direction comes from *Vye*[150] and comprises two limbs: credibility (good character is something which the jury should take into account when deciding whether they believe the defendant's evidence) and propensity (good character may mean that the defendant is less likely to have committed the offence with which he is charged).

The full directions are set out in the Crown Court Compendium at Part 11 and are based on the case of *Hunter*.[151]

There are five categories of good character directions set out in *Hunter*. For practical purposes, categories 3 and 5 might be seen as covering

---

149 Until the Criminal Evidence Act 1898, s.1, a defendant was not allowed to testify in his own defence.

150 *Vye* [1993] 1 WLR 471, [1993] 97 Cr App R 134.

151 Crown Court Compendium Part I, July 2024.

similar ground. The guiding principle for categories 2-5 is that the judge should not give absurd or meaningless directions.

In short:

1. Absolute good character. A good character direction is only compulsory where the defendant "*has no previous convictions or cautions ... and no other reprehensible conduct alleged, admitted or proven*".[152] Failure to give a compulsory good character direction can, depending on "*the nature of the case in question*", result in a conviction being quashed.[153] This is especially so when the central issue is credibility.

2. Effective good character. Where the defendant has some bad character but, in effect, it is trivial and irrelevant to the case,[154] the judge can rule that the defendant should be treated "*as a person of effective good character*" for the purposes of the case. *Hunter* suggests that this is not a purely discretionary exercise; the judge should consider the circumstances and fairness of the situation, and give a reasoned judgment. If so treated, the defendant is entitled to both limbs of the direction, but, depending on the nature of his bad character, the limb(s) may be modified to "*ensure that the jury is not misled*".[155]

3. If the defendant has bad character that he adduces solely for gateway (b) purposes (i.e. no other party relies on it as relevant to the case), the judge has a discretion to give a good character direction,

---

152 *Hunter* [2015] EWCA Crim 631, [2015] 2 Cr App R 9, [77] onwards.

153 See *McChleery* [2019] EWCA Crim 2100, [15].

154 Examples include old class B or C simple drug possession, strict liability road traffic or fare evasion offences, and isolated offences that attracted low-level disposals.

155 For the interaction between a bind-over and a good character direction, see *B(E)* [2017] EWCA Crim 35, [2017] 1 Cr App R 31.

which may be one or both of the limbs modified in any necessary way.[156]

4. Where the jury are told of bad character that is only in the form of non-conviction or non-caution evidence,[157] the judge may accompany the required bad character direction with a modified good character one. This is a "*broad discretion*". However, it is important not to "*neutralise*" the good character direction by over-associating it with the bad character allegations. It is also important to remind the jury that they must give the defendant "*the full benefit of his good character unless they were sure of the bad character allegations*".[158]

5. Where the defendant admits non-conviction[159] reprehensible conduct that is not relied on by the Crown as probative of guilt, the judge may give a modified good character direction. This too is a broad discretion.

Other general principles:

---

156 In *O'Donnell* [2024] EWCA Crim 1115, [35], the defendant "*acknowledged his previous conviction for dishonesty. But he was entitled to present his case on the basis that, notwithstanding that conviction, he had never been involved in violence and was not a violent man.*"

157 These are likely to be of unproved allegations of a similar nature to the current charge.

158 *BQC* [2021] EWCA Crim 1944, [61]-[63].

159 *Hunter* does not say "*no previous convictions* or cautions" as it does for category 4.

- The fact that D2 is not entitled[160] to a good character direction does not affect D1's good character direction.[161] If D1 merits a good character direction, the most that can be done is to direct the jury not to speculate about D2's character. Strategic thinking is needed here, taking into account the context of the case and how the jury might receive such a direction. It may be advisable not to draw further attention to the point.[162]

- D does not have to give evidence in order to benefit from a good character direction. However, the Compendium states that the credibility limb should not be given unless D testifies or has made some out-of-court statement upon which he relies.

- Failure to give the correct good character direction is not fatal, the safety of the conviction depends on the circumstances of the case.[163]

Good character of a non-defendant is treated differently. In *Mader* the Court set out the following principles in relation to prosecution witnesses:

i) Generally, "*evidence is not admissible simply to show that a prosecution witness has a good character in the sense that he or she is a generally truthful person who should be believed*".

[160] Typically, because he has bad character that the jury does not know about.

[161] For the consequences of giving a co-defendant a good character direction that (it later transpired) was not merited, see *Broda* [2015] EWCA Crim 1000.

[162] For an example of directions given in respect of co-defendants, see *Stokes* [2018] EWCA Crim 1350.

[163] For an example where it was fatal when taken with other considerations, see *D* [2021] EWCA Crim 1423. The direction was given in writing but not orally.

ii) "*[E]vidence is admissible if it is relevant to an issue in the trial*" (unless excluded by one of the normal exclusionary rules of evidence; these include powers to "*refuse to admit evidence that will have an unduly prejudicial and less than probative impact upon the jury*").

iii) There is no closed list of issues to which evidence of disposition may be relevant. However, the Court gave two examples:

   a. "*[C]onsent in a trial involving sexual conduct is an issue to which evidence of character or disposition may be relevant.*"

   b. If the defence to a crime of violence is that the defendant was defending himself against an attack from C, "*it is apparent that the non-violent character of the latter is no less relevant as a matter of logic than that of the former*".

iv) "*If admitting evidence on the basis that it is 'issue-relevant', a trial judge should be astute to ensure that the issue to which it is relevant and its limitations are understood by the jury.*" Admitting the evidence should not "*water down the protection provided by the primary obligation upon the prosecution to prove its case and any good character direction that may be given for the defendant.*"[164]

[164] *Mader* [2018] EWCA Crim 2454, [32]-[33].

CHAPTER THREE

SECTION 100 NON-DEFENDANT BAD CHARACTER

Chapter 3 examines the ways in which a non-defendant's bad character can be admitted pursuant to s.100, and who qualifies as a non-defendant for the purposes of the bad character regime.

3.1 Statutory Provisions

"100 Non-defendant's bad character

(1) In criminal proceedings evidence of the bad character of a person other than the defendant is admissible if and only if—

(a) it is important explanatory evidence,

(b) it has substantial probative value in relation to a matter which—

(i) is a matter in issue in the proceedings, and

(ii) is of substantial importance in the context of the case as a whole, or

(c) all parties to the proceedings agree to the evidence being admissible.

(2) For the purposes of subsection (1)(a) evidence is important explanatory evidence if—

(a) without it, the court or jury would find it impossible or difficult properly to understand other evidence in the case, and

(b) its value for understanding the case as a whole is substantial.

(3) In assessing the probative value of evidence for the purposes of subsection (1)(b) the court must have regard to the following factors (and to any others it considers relevant)—

> *(a) the nature and number of the events, or other things, to which the evidence relates;*
>
> *(b) when those events or things are alleged to have happened or existed;*
>
> *(c) where—*
>
> > *(i) the evidence is evidence of a person's misconduct, and*
> >
> > *(ii) it is suggested that the evidence has probative value by reason of similarity between that misconduct and other alleged misconduct,*
>
> *the nature and extent of the similarities and the dissimilarities between each of the alleged instances of misconduct;*
>
> *(d) where—*
>
> > *(i) the evidence is evidence of a person's misconduct,*
> >
> > *(ii) it is suggested that that person is also responsible for the misconduct charged, and*
> >
> > *(iii) the identity of the person responsible for the misconduct charged is disputed,*
>
> *the extent to which the evidence shows or tends to show that the same person was responsible each time.*

(4) Except where subsection (1)(c) applies, evidence of the bad character of a person other than the defendant must not be given without leave of the court."

Section 100 only applies if s.98(a) or (b) do not. The same definition of bad character evidence applies (see Chapter 2).

3.2 Procedure

An application must be made (unless using s.100(1)(c)). Bad character evidence of a non-defendant cannot be admitted without leave of the court: s.100(4). This is in contrast to the s.101 procedure of 'notice'.

The application must be made as soon as reasonably practicable; and in any event not more than 10 business days after the prosecutor discloses material on which the application is based (if the prosecutor is not the applicant): Crim PR r.21.3(3).

A successful prosecution application to admit evidence under s.100 can still be subject to s.78 of PACE and the evidence excluded.

Section 109 (assumption of truth) applies equally to bad character evidence against a non-defendant.[1]

Note that a person who was originally a co-defendant (D2) but has, before trial, been dealt with another way (e.g. entered an acceptable plea and awaits sentence pending the conclusion of D1's trial on the same or related charges) is *not* a co-defendant for the purposes of D1's trial.[2] Thus, an application (by prosecution or D1) to adduce evidence of D2's bad character must be made under s.100, not s.101. D2's guilty plea to offences arising out of the same facts of the offence with which D1 is charged may be admissible via s.98(a) (see Chapter 2).

There is no requirement that the subject of the bad character evidence be a witness at the trial or otherwise give evidence in any way. In *RA*, the subject of the bad character evidence, C's sister, did not give evidence in

---

1 *AM* [2009] EWCA Crim 618, [22], *Conn* [2018] EWCA Crim 1752.

2 *Jukes* [2018] EWCA Crim 176; *Bogdanovic* [2020] EWCA Crim 1229.

the case. The relevance of the bad character was that the sister had previously had a relationship with D, and that a number of issues arising out of that relationship may have provided evidence of a motive for C making a false accusation.[3]

3.3 The S.100 Gateways

There are three gateways under s.100. Each can be used by any party. The exclusionary provisions and standard of proof differ depending on which party has made the application (see Chapters 5 and 6).

3.3.1 Gateway 100(1)(a)

> *"(a) it is important explanatory evidence"*

Gateway 100(1)(a) is equivalent to 101(1)(c): important explanatory evidence.

The definition of this in s.100(2) is the same as that in s.102 (which supplements 101(1)(c)). The broad approach to the interpretation and application of "*important explanatory evidence*" is therefore the same. See Chapter 4 gateway (c) discussion.

There are few cases clearly applying s.100(1)(a). These tend to show that applications under s.100(1)(a) are often unsuccessful.[4] One reason for this may be the absence of any exclusionary provision if the evidence is admitted at the defendant's behest. The Court of Appeal has therefore said that the risk of satellite litigation is something that a court can

---

3 *RA* [2017] EWCA Crim 1515.

4 See, e.g., *Bogdanovic* [2020] EWCA Crim 1229; *Lee* [2019] EWCA Crim 2052; *Edwards* [2018] EWCA Crim 424.

properly take into account in deciding whether the conditions for admissibility in s.100 have been met.[5]

A successful case is *Luckett*, where the defendant was charged with offences of robbery and putting a person in fear of violence by harassment. Witnesses gave evidence of C's injuries on several occasions. The defendant sought to rely on evidence that C was a drug user who had suffered his injuries during encounters with drug dealers. The Court of Appeal held that this evidence was admissible under s.100(1)(b) or, alternatively, s.100(1)(a): "*the circumstances in which he was said to be associated with persons who might want to do him harm was important explanatory evidence within section 100(1)(a).*"[6] The Court reiterated that the decision on admissibility must be approached on the assumption that the bad character evidence is true (s.109).[7] The importance of the defence assertions to the defence case was such that the conviction was unsafe.

The s.100 gateways are not always clearly distinguished from each other when being used. Thus, in *Dizaei*, the wording of both (a) and (b) was amalgamated in the following explanation of (b):

> *"When it is assessing the probative value of the evidence in accordance with s.100(1)(b) and s.100(3), and consistently with s.100(2), among the factors relevant to the admissibility judgment, the court should reflect whether the admission of the evidence relating to the bad character of the witness might make it difficult for the jury to understand the remainder of the evidence, and whether its understanding of the case as a whole might be diminished. In such cases the conclusion may be that the evidence is not of substantial probative value in establishing the propensity in or lack of credit worthiness of the witness, or that the evidence is not of substantial importance in*

5 *Dizaei* [2013] EWCA Crim 88, [2013] 1 Cr App R 31, [35]. For exclusionary provisions see Chapter 5.

6 *Luckett* [2015] EWCA Crim 1050, [22].

7 *Luckett* [2015] EWCA Crim 1050, [26]-[27].

> *the context of the case as a whole, or both. If so, the pre-conditions to admissibility will not established."*[8]

In one of the *Renda* appeals,[9] it is unclear whether (a) or (b) was being engaged. The defendant was charged with robbery from the till of a pub. He wanted to adduce evidence about the character of the licensee of the pub, C. The judge admitted bad character allegations concerning general till shortages and the provision of free drink, because these lent support to the allegation that any shortage in the till might be attributed to C's misconduct, rather than the alleged robbery. However, the judge refused to admit allegations that C used drugs, as the allegation that the premises were misused generally for drug offences did not help to demonstrate why or support the conclusion that C was or may have been inventing a fictitious crime.

3.3.2 Gateway 100(1)(b)

> *"(b) it has substantial probative value in relation to a matter which—*
>
> > *(i) is a matter in issue in the proceedings, and*
> >
> > *(ii) is of substantial importance in the context of the case as a whole"*

This gateway has common elements with s.101(1)(d) ((important) matter in issue) and s.101(1)(e) (substantial probative value). Be aware that the tests are not the same, and that the words "*matter in issue*" in 100(1)(b)(i) are not necessarily the same as "*important matter in issue*" in s.101(1)(d) and (e), when taken with the definition of "*important matter*" in s.112(1).

---

8 *Dizaei* [2013] EWCA Crim 88, [2013] 1 Cr App R 31, [38].

9 *Renda* [2005] EWCA Crim 2826, [2006] 1 Cr App R 24, [57].

However, the meaning of "*substantial probative value*" is the same in s.100(1)(b)(ii) and s.101(1)(e) (see Chapter 4 gateway (e)). Note, however, that in addition to substantial probative value, s.100(1)(b)(ii) also requires that the matter in issue be of "*substantial importance in the context of the case as a whole*". There are two different "*substantial*" tests to be passed.

In *Braithwaite*, the Court gave a concise overview of how s.100(1)(b) is intended to work.[10]

1. The test of "*substantial probative value*" is higher[11] than the test for gateway (d). There the test is whether the evidence is "*relevant*". It is, however, the same as appears in gateway (e). "*The expression has been referred to in some quarters as importing a test of 'enhanced probative value'.*"

2. The assessment is "*highly fact-sensitive*". "*It is an assessment of whether the evidence in question* substantially *goes to show (prove) the point which the applicant wishes to prove on the issue in question.*"

3. "*The issue will often, but not always, be either the propensity of the person against whom the application is made to behave in a particular way, or his credibility.*"

4. Section 100(3) contains a non-exhaustive list of factors that are relevant to assessing the probative value of the bad character evidence. These are largely self-explanatory. Paragraphs (c) and (d) primarily concern the suggestion that someone else is or may be responsible for the criminality with which the defendant is currently charged. Thus, the factors point to the extent of any similarity to other alleged misconduct if that is said to be the source

10 *Braithwaite* [2010] EWCA (Crim) 1082, [2010] 2 Cr App R 18, [12]-[16], now refined in *BVY* [2024] EWCA Crim 1355.

11 *BVY* [2024] EWCA Crim 1355, [29](i).

of its probative value and, *"if it be suggested that the evidence is such as shows that the non-defendant committed the offence being tried, the extent to which the totality of the evidence tends to show that the same person was responsible for both the bad character event and the offence being tried."* Section 100(3) *"emphasises that the test of substantial probative value is a test of the force of the evidence which it is sought to adduce."*

5. There is no residual discretion to refuse to admit if s.100(1)(b) is satisfied, consequently the threshold for admissibility is the only safeguard (although s.78 still applies to prosecution evidence).

As noted in *Dizaei*, the considerations under s.100(2) may be incorporated into s.100(3) decisions where appropriate.[12]

There is no statutory restriction on what kind of bad character is admissible under s.100(1)(b). The gateway is not restricted, for example, to evidence of the making of false statements:

> *"It does not follow, as we have held, that previous convictions which do not involve either the making of false statements or the giving of false evidence, are incapable of having substantial probative value in relation to the credibility of a non-defendant under section 100, or for that matter of a co-accused where the application is made by him under section 101(1)(e)."*[13]

However, avoiding satellite litigation is relevant when assessing the question of substantial probative value.[14] In *Umo*, applying s.109 there was a "*clear basis*" for the conclusion that allegations against a witness were properly substantiated. There was no risk of the jury "*embarking on a second simultaneous trial*", which might have deprived the evidence of the

12 *Dizaei* [2013] EWCA Crim 88, [2013] 1 Cr App R 31, [30].

13 *Stephenson* [2006] EWCA Crim 2325, [27].

14 *King* [2015] EWCA Crim 1631, [40], [41], [55].

requisite substantial probative value. The evidence should have been admitted, and the convictions were therefore quashed.[15]

Bare allegations are less likely to be admissible under s.100(1)(b). In *Bovell and Dowds* the Court of Appeal said: "*we entertain considerable doubt as to whether the mere making of an allegation is capable of being evidence within section 100(1).*"[16] However, in *Lawrence*, the Court held that the complainant's credibility was in issue. And both convictions and allegations about her honesty were admissible under s.100(1)(b).[17]

3.3.2.1 Section 100(1)(b) and Loss of Shield (Gateway (g))

Defendants should be wary of waiting for their bad character to be admitted before seeking to rely on the bad character evidence of a prosecution witness. In *Myers*, the prosecution successfully adduced the defendant's bad character via gateway (d). The defendant then applied to admit evidence of C's convictions, under s.100(1)(b), on the basis that C's accusations against the defendant had been made in retaliation for the defendant publicising C's convictions to others. The defendant had not raised this defence before, arguing instead that C was mistaken in his identification of the defendant as the perpetrator.

The judge refused the defendant's application, noting that the circumstances in which the application arose indicated that there was no real matter in issue in the proceedings of substantial importance in the context of the case as a whole, such as to give to those convictions substantial probative value. The essence of the defence argument seemed to be that

---

15 *Umo* [2020] EWCA Crim 284, [38]

16 *Bovell and Dowds* [2005] EWCA Crim 1091, [2005] 2 Cr App R 27, [21]. See also *Renda* [2005] EWCA Crim 2826, [2006] 1 Cr App R 24, [46].

17 *Lawrence* [2012] EWCA Crim 2144. See more recently *A* [2020] EWCA Crim 1687.

"*it was only fair that if the jury were to know about the appellant's convictions, then they should equally know about the complainant's convictions*".[18] This does not satisfy s.100(1)(b).

It appears that, had C's motivations been raised in the defence statement, the position may have been different. The Court did note that, in general, the desire not to lose his shield pre-emptively might be a good reason for the defendant not making such an application until his own bad character had been admitted. Had there been more than a merely speculative basis for the allegation about C's motivations, the evidence may have been admissible.[19]

3.3.2.2 Character of Police Officers

Gaiziunas involved the discovery that a police officer, who claimed to have found a knife in the defendant's possession, had subsequently been convicted of assault and perverting the course of justice (apparently assisted by other officers) during the course of an unrelated arrest. Police disciplinary proceedings had also resulted in further findings against the officer, both pre-dating the defendant's arrest and in relation to the defendant's own arrest. The defendant's case at trial had been that the knife had been put into his bag by someone else, and he questioned why the other officers present had not made statements. When this information subsequently came to light, the Court of Appeal had no hesitation in quashing the conviction and agreeing that this bad character evidence was admissible under s.100(1)(b).[20]

---

18 *Myers* [2010] EWCA Crim 3173, [25].

19 But see *Stapleton* [2014] EWCA Crim 1983.

20 *Gaiziunas* [2024] EWCA Crim 246.

3.3.2.3 Non-Defendant Gang Evidence

In *Abdirahman*, the trial judge had been right to allow evidence that H, the defendant's brother, was associated with members of a gang. This evidence undermined the defence that the defendant was unaware of what was happening on the night in question, and was unaware of any gang related animosity. It was not, however, s.100(1)(a) "*important explanatory evidence*" because it was not necessary to enable the jury to understand the case against the defendant. It was s.100(1)(b) evidence, because it went to the defendant's awareness of the ongoing gang disputes. Section 78 did not assist because, "*it is difficult to see that the material was of any significant prejudicial effect so far as [D] was concerned. It comprised criminal associations of his brother, not him.*"[21] Of course, this has to be considered against the probative value of the material, which was only admissible in the first place because it went to show the defendant's association with his brother.

3.3.2.4 Self-Defence and Non-Defendant Bad Character

Evidence that a complainant has a violent character can be relevant to whether the defendant has acted in self-defence. It is a necessary corollary of the principle in *Mader*,

> "*If the accused's defence to a charge of some crime of violence is that he was defending himself against an attack launched by the complainant, it is apparent that the non-violent character of the latter is no less relevant as a matter of logic than that of the former.*"[22]

The succinct decision in *Afolabi* must, it is submitted, be considered an outlier. There, D was convicted of wounding with intent to cause grievous bodily harm. The complainant C did not give evidence. The Crown's

21 *Abdirahman* [2021] EWCA Crim 1935, [28].

22 *Mader* [2018] EWCA Crim 2454, and see above under Good Character.

case relied upon agreed medical evidence of the wounds sustained by C and CCTV showing much of the event. D asserted that C was the aggressor, had come towards him armed with a knife, and in the ensuing struggle C had been injured (it is undeniable that there were clear inconsistencies in D's accounts). He sought to rely upon an allegation that C had stabbed D some 4 months after this event. The prosecution said this would be satellite litigation because the defendant (like C in this trial) had failed to give evidence at C's trial in respect of that allegation and consequently the trial could not proceed. The Court dismissed the appeal, stating "*Even if [D] was stabbed by the victim, the stabbing postdated [D's] offence by a significant period. Evidence of the stabbing could cast no light on any issue that the jury had to decide in the applicant's trial.*"[23]

It may be that this case turns on its specific facts and what could be seen on the CCTV. Otherwise, it might be hard to see how evidence of a violent attack by C upon the defendant just four months later does not satisfy s.100(1)(b). Section 109(1) would apply (s.109(2) being a rarely invoked and high threshold), and as C had not attended to give evidence it might be thought that the risk of satellite litigation was minimal. As discussed in Chapter 5, bad character can post-date the relevant offending as well as pre-date it.

3.3.2.5 Section 41 and Non-Defendant Bad Character

In the event that evidence of sexual behaviour falling under s.41 of the Youth Justice and Criminal Evidence Act 1991 could reasonably also be described as bad character evidence, both s.100 and s.41 need to be satisfied (see 112(3)(b)).[24] However, accusations that C has made *false*

23 *Afolabi* [2024] EWCA Crim 249, [13]. The Court went so far as to make a loss of time order against the defendant.

24 E.g., *Smith* [2017] EWCA Crim 941, [21]-[22].

allegations of sexual abuse against other persons do not fall within s.41; only s.100 would need to be satisfied (see below 3.3.2.6).[25]

The interaction between s.41 and s.100 was examined in *Wilson*. In short, if evidence satisfies s.100(1)(b), "*then it is likely that its exclusion would fall foul of section 41(2)(b) and it would be admitted*". This is because the wording of s.41(2)(b) "*must include a test which amounts to the same thing*" as s.100(1)(b). "*It would be incoherent to have different tests in provisions which are designed to achieve related objectives.*"[26]

3.3.2.6 Complainant's Propensity to Make False Allegations

In the context of a complainant's allegedly false allegations, s.109 requires "*some material from which it could properly conclude that the complaint was false*".[27] In *Gabbai*, the judge was wrong to have excluded evidence of previous false complaints by C:

> *"In our view, this evidence was of a striking nature, and relevant as suggestive of previous false accounts. The evidence that the complainant had doubted her own past suggestions of rape ... should have been admitted pursuant to s.100 CJA 2003. This provided an evidential foundation for a conclusion of falsity, of substantial importance in the case as a whole, and should have been before the jury."*[28]
>
> *"Had this evidence been admitted, the interpretation of the [video of the alleged rape] might very easily have been affected. As we have*

25 *Stephenson* [2006] EWCA Crim 2325; *Clarke* [2016] EWCA Crim 2030.

26 *Wilson* [2024] EWCA Crim 1514, [41].

27 *AM* [2009] EWCA Crim 618, [22]; see also *Conn* [2018] EWCA Crim 1752; *Knight* [2013] EWCA Crim 2486.

28 *Gabbai* [2019] EWCA Crim 2287, [2020] 4 WLR 65, [59].

> *said, the video evidence is key as it is in apparent conflict with the account of [C]. That was properly a matter for the jury."*[29]

However, an allegation is not false merely because no charges were brought in respect of it.[30]

The lapse of time is a relevant factor: in *CB*, an allegation that the complainant had made a false complaint some 10 years earlier (when she was aged 12) was not admissible.[31]

In *Hussain* (2015), C's general creditworthiness was in issue and her convictions were so numerous, varied and recent that they were of substantial probative value upon the issue of whether her accusation against the defendant was worthy of belief. They should have been left to the jury, whose task it was to decide whether they assisted in resolving who was telling the truth.[32]

A similar conclusion was reached in *Hussain* (2021). A key prosecution witness had convictions for dishonesty, perverting the course of justice, and offending arising from the underlying hostility between the defendant's and witness's families. These were admissible as going to the witness's credibility, level of involvement in the ongoing dispute, and propensity and motivation falsely to implicate someone else, in this case the defendant. While some of the lesser convictions may not individually have been sufficiently probative, taken together they had a clear potential to have a "*significant impact on the standing of the witness*".[33] The

[29] *Gabbai* [2019] EWCA Crim 2287, [2020] 4 WLR 65, [64].

[30] *Simpson* [2021] EWCA Crim 302

[31] *CB* [2020] EWCA Crim 790, [106].

[32] *Hussain* [2015] EWCA Crim 383, [24]. C's convictions were many and varied: see [7].

[33] *Hussain* [2021] EWCA Crim 870, [34]. One reason for the problems that arose in this case was the piecemeal way in which detail of the witness's convictions had been produced.

circumstances of the convictions were readily available, could be agreed, and would not have resulted in satellite litigation. The conviction was quashed.

By way of contrast see *ABY*, where the Court of Appeal was unpersuaded that the defendant's conviction was unsafe following the discovery of material which, in the CCRC's view, "*substantially undermined*" C's credibility.[34]

In *Moody*, the suggestion (in school records, not by way of conviction) that the complainant "*was capable of expressing racist language (more than once)*" might have been admissible as going to her credibility and motivation to accuse the defendant.[35]

In *Livesey*,[36] the defendant was charged with drug supply offences and had been found in possession of an address book containing (amongst others) names and details of persons who had convictions of drug dealing. Those convictions were admissible under s.100(1)(b).

3.3.2.7 An Alternative Suspect for the Offending

In *Mohammed*, DNA evidence obtained years after conviction showed that another individual, S, might in fact be responsible for the indecent assaults with which the defendant was charged. S had a caution which the Court of Appeal said was admissible pursuant to s.100(1)(b), as going "*not to propensity, but to rebuttal of a coincidence.*" That coincidence was that there was another man who happened to satisfy a number of features that the prosecution said implicated the defendant. The caution had

34 *Aby* [2024] EWCA Crim 944.

35 *Moody* [2019] EWCA Crim 1222, [23].

36 *Livesey* [2019] EWCA Crim 877.

substantial probative value because it demonstrated that S, and his other offending, had the potential to or did bear these same features.[37]

3.3.3 Gateway 100(1)(c)

> *"(c) all parties to the proceedings agree to the evidence being admissible."*

This is the equivalent of s.101(1)(a). It is self-explanatory and unlikely to cause difficulty. Leave of the court is not required. Note that the agreement required is from all *parties* to the proceedings (i.e. prosecutor and all defendants). The subject of the bad character evidence is not required to agree. Indeed there is no statutory requirement to consult the non-defendant.

Usually, an agreed fact pursuant to s.10 of the Criminal Justice Act 1967 will be the most appropriate method. The evidence can also be elicited via the officer in the case or an equivalent witness who is familiar with the facts. Care should be taken to restrict the witness's answers to agreed material; inadvertently revealing more than is necessary can result in legal argument about complicated jury directions or, in severe cases, discharge of the jury. If the inadvertent material is elicited on behalf of a defendant, it could result in a prosecution application under gateway (g).

---

37 *Mohammed* [2021] EWCA Crim 201, [43].

CHAPTER FOUR

SECTION 101 DEFENDANT BAD CHARACTER

Chapter 4 deals with the main focus of the bad character regime: the gateways under s.101. Each gateway is examined in turn, breaking down the elements required for each and providing a quick reference to key cases for issues that arise. There is particular focus on the substantive gateways and especially gateway (d). The Chapter looks at the meaning of often-used phrases like 'important explanatory evidence', 'important matter in issue', the application of the *Hanson* principles, 'substantial probative value', 'false impression' and 'attacks' on the character of others.

4.1 Gateway (a): S.101(1)(a)

> *"(a) all parties to the proceedings agree to the evidence being admissible"*

As with its counterpart s.100(1)(c) (non-defendant agreed bad character), this is self-explanatory and unlikely to cause difficulty.

"*All parties*" means all defendants and the prosecution; agreement between the prosecution and the defendant whose character under discussion will not suffice.[1]

This gateway is not an invitation to distract the jury with peripheral or unnecessary detail. If the evidence is not relevant the judge is entitled to

1 *Ferdinand* [2014] EWCA Crim 1243, [2014] 2 Cr App R 23.

enquire more closely of the parties how its admission will assist the jury.[2] It may also be prudent to make enquiries where a defendant is unrepresented.

Usually, an agreed fact pursuant to s.10 of the Criminal Justice Act 1967 will be the most appropriate method. The court should be informed before the agreed evidence is placed before the jury.

The evidence can be elicited via the officer in the case or an equivalent witness who is familiar with the facts. Care should be taken to restrict the witness's answers to agreed material; inadvertently revealing more than is necessary can result in legal argument about complicated jury directions or, in severe cases, discharge of the jury. If the inadvertent material is elicited on behalf of a defendant, it could result in a prosecution application under gateway (g).

The intent behind gateways (a) and (b) is to allow bad character evidence to be used only with the defendant's consent.

However, it is clear that once a defendant agrees to let his character in, it can be used by any party for any relevant purpose with or without his consent. Defendants should also be aware that once evidence has been admitted, via any gateway, it can be used by any party for any relevant purpose (see *Highton* discussed at gateway (g) below).

In *Cundell* the defendant was convicted of soliciting someone to murder his wife. He had previously pleaded guilty to an earlier charge of soliciting the murder of his wife. While in prison for that offence, he met X, whom he asked to kill his wife. This was the subject of the present charge.

The previous conviction was admitted by consent under gateway (a). Both parties agreed it was relevant to the background of these allegations

---

2 *Reid* [2024] EWCA Crim 308, [42].

which could not be explained without reference to the conviction.[3] However the judge then gave a propensity direction in relation to the conviction. It does not appear that the defendant appreciated the effect of *Highton* here. It did not matter much in this particular case, because it is difficult not to agree with the Court of Appeal's conclusion that the conviction was safe: "*[i]t seems to us hard to imagine a case in which the previous conviction could be more relevant to 'an important matter in issue between the prosecution and the defence.'*"[4] A clearer example of propensity under gateway (d) would be hard to find.

For a similar situation in the gateway (b) context, see *Tollady*. It was taken for granted that using gateway (b) bad character evidence for a s.103(1)(a)-type purpose was unquestionably correct in the circumstances. It was not correct to use it for a s.103(1)(b)-type purpose (i.e. credibility), but because the bad character evidence had originally been admitted at the defendant's own instigation, there were no adverse consequences in this case.[5] The case illustrates the caution that a defendant should exercise before agreeing to let his character into evidence.

4.2 Gateway (b): S.101(1)(b)

> *"(b) the evidence is adduced by the defendant himself or is given in answer to a question asked by him in cross-examination and intended to elicit it"*

---

3 *Cundell* [2009] EWCA Crim 2072, [53]. Although it may be queried, by analogy with the gateway (c) argument (see later in this Chapter) whether the nature of the defendant's conviction needed to be revealed, or merely the fact that he was in prison for an unspecified crime.

4 *Cundell* [2009] EWCA Crim 2072, [56].

5 *Tollady* [2010] EWCA Crim 2614, [26].

Again, this is generally uncontroversial. A defendant is entitled to put his own character into evidence, and judges will generally allow considerable latitude in relation to the relevance of such material.

Possible reasons for using gateway (b) include:

- Showing that D has always pleaded guilty to previous offences, and therefore is truthful and willing to accept when he has done something wrong.
- Showing that D has relatively minor convictions/cautions that bear no resemblance to the current matter. This can lead to a modified good character direction: see Chapter 2.
- Drawing a distinction between D1's own character and that of a co-defendant (D2) with more serious convictions. This is a bold move, but if D2's convictions are of such probative value that they would satisfy gateway (e), D1 may wish to agree to his convictions being put into evidence via gateway (b) rather than have them ruled in under gateway (g) in retaliation for attacking D2's character.
- Placing a conviction into context (for example, if the prosecution has already successfully adduced evidence of one conviction to show a propensity).
- Showing that a witness has a motive to dislike or falsely accuse the defendant because of his convictions.

Defendants should be cautious of using gateway (b) in such a way as to give a false impression that would trigger gateway (f).

A defendant who wants to use gateway (b) must at the latest give notice prior to the evidence being introduced (CPR r.21.4(8)). While there is no mechanism to object or exclude this evidence (save perhaps a baseline rule of relevance to the trial), gateway (b) is not a 'surprise' gateway.

As with gateway (a), defendants should also be aware that once evidence has been admitted, via any gateway, it can be used by any party for any relevant purpose (see above under gateway (a), and *Highton* discussed at gateway (g) below).

4.3 Gateway (c): S.101(1)(c)

> *"(c) it is important explanatory evidence"*

"102 'Important explanatory evidence'

For the purposes of section 101(1)(c) evidence is important explanatory evidence if—

> *(a) without it, the court or jury would find it impossible or difficult properly to understand other evidence in the case, and*
>
> *(b) its value for understanding the case as a whole is substantial."*

4.3.1 Scope Of Application

Gateway (c) is available to any party. It is not restricted to prosecution evidence.

For the overlap between gateway (c), s.98(a) and res gestae, see Chapter 2.

Section 102 sets a high threshold for "*important explanatory evidence*".[6]

The key question is whether other evidence already in the case is not capable of being understood and requires explanation. This is a narrow application.

---

6 *Beverley* [2006] EWCA Crim 1287, *Saint* [2010] EWCA Crim 1924, *Broome* [2012] EWCA Crim 2879.

In particular, care should be taken to separate it from gateway (d): "*It is not possible to dress up a failed case of gateway (d) as gateway (c)*".[7] The gateway should be "*applied cautiously where it is argued to overlap with a submitted case of propensity*".[8]

Satellite litigation (although less likely in the (c) context) should be guarded against.[9]

In *Saint*, the defendant was convicted (in 2009) of false imprisonment, two indecent assaults, and rape against C, occurring on the same night in a car park in 1989. The judge admitted bad character evidence via gateway (c) to the effect that several years later, in the mid-1990s, the defendant visited that car park at night, dressed in camouflage and with a military specification night-sight. He had demonstrated an interest in watching couples having sexual intercourse. This bad character evidence was said to explain "*other evidence*" in the case, being evidence from a friend of C's who had been with her prior to the attack, that he had heard footsteps while he was with her.

The Court of Appeal disagreed:

> *"The evidence it was said to explain was the evidence, mainly from [the friend who had just left C], about footsteps [he heard when opening the car door]. That evidence was not impossible or difficult to understand. On the contrary, it was readily intelligible. Its deficiency was that the Crown could not identify the footsteps with [D]. Nor, in our view, could they readily do so by resort to the bad character*

7 *D, P and U* [2011] EWCA Crim 1474, [2012] 1 Cr App R 8, [22].

8 *Davis* [2008] EWCA Crim 1156, [2009] 2 Cr App R 17, [36].

9 *Edwards and Rowlands* [2005] EWCA Crim 3244, [2006] 2 Cr App R 4, [86], and *O'Dowd* [2009] EWCA Crim 905, [2009] 2 Cr App R 16.

> *evidence, not least because it all related to a time four or five years or more after 5 January 1989."*[10]

Temporally distant bad character evidence is not usually admissible under gateway (c). See Chapter 5 for a discussion of lapse of time.

One exception is where a party seeks to use background relationship evidence to explain the relationship between two parties at the time of the present charge.

In *P*, the defendant was charged with the rape of his girlfriend. The girlfriend also alleged that the defendant had on six previous occasions been violent towards her, and, on a seventh occasion, had raped her (a different rape allegation from the one on the indictment). These seven incidents were admissible under (c). It was in fact the "*nature of the defence*" that made this necessary.[11] The defendant had given his account of their relationship. The complainant's account was therefore necessary before the jury could understand the relationship.[12]

---

10 *Saint* [2010] EWCA Crim 1924, [16]. In general, the lapse of time affects admissibility because of the nature of the gateway. See, e.g., *Davis* [2008] EWCA Crim 1156, [2009] 2 Cr App R 17, where evidence of 20 years ago could not possibly have any important explanatory effect on the present crime; the case of *Smith* in *Edwards and Rowlands* [2005] EWCA Crim 3244, [2006] 2 Cr App R 4, where evidence about events within a few years but not about the events charged was not admissible under gateway (c).

11 It would be "*unfair to the prosecution*" not to be allowed to adduce the bad character evidence: *P* [2006] EWCA Crim 2517, [7].

12 The relationship being a "*central issue in the case*" also meant that the evidence was admissible under gateway (d).

It is questionable whether bad character evidence providing a "*factual backdrop*" is enough.[13]

See *Hackett*, where the defendant was charged with a sexual assault on a particular occasion. The judge admitted evidence of a history of "*abuse and aggression*" by the defendant towards C, under a number of gateways including (c), (d), (f), and (g). The exact basis was unclear. The Court of Appeal said that none of the evidence should have been admitted under s.101, "*as it was irrelevant, prejudicial and such probative value as it contained was significantly outweighed by its prejudicial nature*". Recognising that there would need to be some reference to the history of the relationship, any background evidence that was properly admissible should have been subject to limits.[14] Care should be taken to identify and enforce the uses of the bad character evidence:

> *"In our view if a judge is minded to permit evidence to be adduced as to background evidence it is incumbent upon the judge when ruling upon admissibility, to identify the reasons for its admission, the parameters of such evidence, how it can be used, in particular what can be said by any witness as to that evidence, whether it be in examination-in-chief or the extent of any cross-examination, and in that ruling to give an indication of how the jury will subsequently be directed upon that evidence. In this case that was not done. The brief and somewhat general ruling of the judge appears to have permitted prosecuting counsel to embark upon a cross-examination, untrammelled by judicial intervention, which not only went beyond the ruling of the judge, it entered into areas of evidence which were peripheral, irrelevant and prejudicial to the defendant. Put shortly,*

---

13 *Lowe* [2007] EWCA Crim 3047, [13]. See also *Gillespie* [2011] EWCA Crim 3152; *Iqbal* [2006] EWCA Crim 1302; *Jalland* [2006] EWCA Crim 3336; *Kesseidou* [2005] EWCA Crim 2931; *Osbourne* [2007] EWCA Crim 481.

14 *Hackett* [2019] EWCA Crim 983, [41]-[42].

> *having provided a brief and general ruling, the judge failed thereafter to provide any effective management of the use of such evidence.* [15]

If the real reason for adducing the evidence is to make one's case stronger or rebut the opposite case, then gateway (c) is not available.[16]

In *Beverley*, it was not disputed that there was a conspiracy to import cocaine, but the question was whether the defendant was a knowing participant. He had two previous convictions (both guilty pleas), one for possession of cannabis with intent to supply and one for simple possession of cannabis. The Court of Appeal held that the conditions in s.102 were not satisfied. Even if ignorant of the prior convictions, the jury would not have been disadvantaged in understanding any of the evidence allegedly connecting the defendant with the crime. "*The evidence was perfectly clear. It required no footnote or lexicon.*"[17] The real reason for the prosecution's desire to admit the convictions was to make it more likely that the jury would disbelieve the defendant's story. Gateway (c) is not relevant to such motives.

> *"The Crown's true position is that evidence of these convictions might make it more likely that the jury would disbelieve the appellant's account. That might or might not be the fact of the matter, but it has nothing whatever to do with the gateway at section 101(1)(c) as interpreted in section 102. There should never have been an application under section 101(1)(c) in this case nor should it have been supported here. The gateway at section 101(1)(c) was entirely unavailable."*[18]

15 *Hackett* [2019] EWCA Crim 983, [43].

16 See e.g. *Iqbal* [2006] EWCA Crim 1302, but cf *P* [2006] EWCA Crim 2517.

17 *Beverley* [2006] EWCA Crim 1287, [7].

18 *Beverley* [2006] EWCA Crim 1287, [7].

The value of the bad character evidence for understanding the case as a whole must be substantial. The volumes of evidence admitted in *Doncaster* should be avoided where possible.[19] There, evidence of three enquiries over 17 years was admissible under gateway (c) to explain charges arising only out of the last enquiry.

Section 102 precludes the admission of bad character evidence to explain "*other evidence*" that plays a minor or peripheral role in the case.

It also precludes the admission of evidence that simply satisfies curiosity or enquiry as to the nature of the 'whole picture'. Gateway (c) cannot be used simply to fill a lacuna in the picture before the jury.[20]

Gateway (c) and gang evidence.

Evidence associating a person with a gang can be gateway (c) evidence. In *Okokono*,[21] the defendant was convicted of a gang-related murder, allegedly committed in retaliation for the murder of a member of his own gang 18 months earlier. The defendant had pleaded guilty to possessing a knife, on the night of his friend's murder, at a location not far from the location of his friend's murder.

The Court of Appeal said that this conviction showed two things: (1) that D was a party to the attack seeking to avenge the death of his friend in a gang-related feud which he may have triggered; and (2) D's realisation that a knife or knives might be used with lethal intent if gang violence broke out. It was evidence showing the true nature and extent of D's connection to the death of his friend and his affiliation to his gang. Without it there was a danger that the jury would be materially misled as to the nature and significance of D's connections with what had gone on.

---

19 *Doncaster* [2008] EWCA Crim 5.

20 *Lee* [2012] EWCA Crim 316, endorsed in *Grundell* [2024] EWCA Crim 364.

21 *Okokono* [2014] EWCA Crim 2521.

The exact means by which the conviction was admissible was unclear. The Court said:[22]

1) It was admissible under s.98 as highly relevant evidence of the background to the killing of the victim in the present charge, and it was therefore to do with the facts of the case.

2) It was also admissible as important explanatory evidence under s.101(c) to explain the motive for the murder, namely a revenge attack.

3) It was admissible under s.101(d) to establish D's willingness to engage in gang fights, knowing that others had a propensity to use knives to lethal effect. See also gateway (d) below on gang-association evidence.

The reasoning at (2) still requires the criteria for gateway (c) to be satisfied. Evidence explaining a motive does not necessarily satisfy s.102(a). Lack of evidence of a motive does not mean the jury will have difficulty in understanding what the prosecution alleges (i.e. the elements of the actual offence charged). It may mean that the jury are not *convinced* of what the prosecution alleges, but that is a different problem altogether and one that is not necessarily supposed to be solved by the admission of bad character.

4.3.2 How Much Evidence Is Needed?

The existence of bad character evidence is often incidental to the purpose for which important explanatory evidence is admitted. That is, some evidence may be needed to explain principal evidence in the case, but it does not follow that any and all associated bad character evidence need

22 *Okokono* [2014] EWCA Crim 2521, [60].

be revealed. It can be sanitised or limited so as to reduce any unnecessary prejudicial effect.[23]

There are, of course, those cases where failure to specify the bad character details might lead to undesirable jury speculation about the bowdlerised evidence. In such cases, full disclosure might be more desirable,[24] or s.78 might provide an appropriate solution.

An example of a case that readily satisfies the need for bad character to be revealed is *Johnson*.[25] D1 was convicted of importing cocaine and cannabis, while D2 (a former girlfriend) was acquitted. At the time of the events in question, D2 had complained of common assault by D1, and the police were investigating. She later dropped the complaint. The fact of the complaint was admissible via gateway (c) because "*it gave an explanation … for the co-accused to lie to the police that she had arrived at the depot by bus.*"[26] She lied because, as she later admitted, she did not want the police to know that D1 had driven her there; she was not meant to be with him while her complaint of common assault was investigated. This, it is suggested, is very much the sort of situation that gateway (c) is intended to remedy. Importantly, it was the *fact* of the complaint and not the alleged common assault itself that was being used, and this was made clear to the jury.

---

23 Indeed, this can be done in relation to any presentation of bad character evidence: see *Awoyemi* [2016] EWCA Crim 668, [37].

24 See, e.g., *Dabycharun* [2021] EWCA Crim 1923, [29].

25 Gateway (c) would also have been appropriate in *Lewis* [2008] EWCA Crim 424, where the Court instead applied gateway (f) to bad character evidence adduced by a co-defendant.

26 *Johnson* [2007] EWCA Crim 1651.

In contrast, see the selectiveness employed in *Gillhooley*, where only a few parts of the evidence in question needed to be seen by the jury in order that they might appreciate the allegations being made.[27]

In *Shiekh* the defendant was convicted in 2012 of breaching a sexual offences prevention order. The order had been made in 2005 after the defendant was convicted of rape. The judge ruled, using gateway (c),[28] that the jury should be informed of the facts of the rape so that it could understand the terms of the order, although the order already contained a reference to the conviction itself.

The Court of Appeal held that this was in error. The issues did not require the jury to know the prejudicial details of the rape conviction. They merely had to ascertain whether the defendant had infringed the terms of the order—they did not need to know why the order had been made.

> *"They may indeed have speculated about the reason for the making of the order, but that is not a proper basis for adducing evidence under gateway (c). The judge could simply have told the jury that they were not to be concerned as to the reason why the order was imposed and simply accept that it was and to decide whether or not it had been infringed."*[29]

Sanitising the evidence can actually remove the need to use the bad character regime at all.

In *Jalland*, the defendant was convicted of murdering his wife in 2004. The bad character evidence was that the defendant had, in 1996, stolen a Montego car from his employer. The judge allowed this evidence via gateway (c). The sequence of reasoning was as follows:

---

27 *Gillhooley* [2012] EWCA Crim 220, [24].

28 A gateway (d) application was rejected.

29 *Shiekh* [2013] EWCA Crim 907, [9].

(1) Found at the defendant's home were two original keys to his wife's Honda, and three other keys, none original, to the stolen Montego car.

(2) In order to explain that there was a third Honda key that his wife might have used when she disappeared (and therefore without his involvement), the defendant used the existence of the three Montego keys to show that he often got car keys cut.

(3) The prosecution wanted to rebut this by saying that the extra keys for the Montego could be explained by the fact of its theft in 1996. In interview, when asked "*how did you manage to steal the Montego?*", the defendant replied: "*I had the keys, spare keys cut*".

The Court of Appeal said that this was not evidence worthy of gateway (c). "*It is difficult to see how the fact that the Montego was stolen truly explains why three sets of keys to it existed.*"[30] The "*patent irrelevance of stealing a car in 1996 to a charge of murdering one's wife in 2004*" was "*an irrelevance which any jury would have appreciated*".[31] If anything needed to be explained so that the jury could properly understand the existence of non-original keys, it would have been the dates and frequency of the defendant's obtaining such keys, not the motive. Thus, the bad character could be removed from the important explanatory evidence. This would, in fact, render the evidence wholly exempt from the CJA scheme for bad character evidence.

Thus, the relevance of bad character in gateway (c) is actually very limited because the existence of the bad character is incidental to the primary purpose of explanation. It is not being introduced in order to show the bad character itself, unlike gateways (d), (e), (f) and (g). Wherever possible, the bad character should be removed from the admissible evidence where it does not contribute to the reason why evidence X needs

---

30 *Jalland* [2006] EWCA Crim 3336, [25].

31 *Jalland* [2006] EWCA Crim 3336, [29].

explanation. Only where the explanatory evidence happens to be inextricable from bad character evidence should that bad character evidence be admitted.

4.4 Gateway (d): S.101(1)(d)

"(d) it is relevant to an important matter in issue between the defendant and the prosecution"

"103 'Matter in issue between the defendant and the prosecution'

(1) For the purposes of section 101(1)(d) the matters in issue between the defendant and the prosecution include—

> *(a) the question whether the defendant has a propensity to commit offences of the kind with which he is charged, except where his having such a propensity makes it no more likely that he is guilty of the offence;*
>
> *(b) the question whether the defendant has a propensity to be untruthful, except where it is not suggested that the defendant's case is untruthful in any respect.*

(2) Where subsection (1)(a) applies, a defendant's propensity to commit offences of the kind with which he is charged may (without prejudice to any other way of doing so) be established by evidence that he has been convicted of—

> *(a) an offence of the same description as the one with which he is charged, or*
>
> *(b) an offence of the same category as the one with which he is charged.*

(3) Subsection (2) does not apply in the case of a particular defendant if the court is satisfied, by reason of the length of time since the conviction or for any other reason, that it would be unjust for it to apply in his case.

(4) For the purposes of subsection (2)—

> *(a) two offences are of the same description as each other if the statement of the offence in a written charge or indictment would, in each case, be in the same terms;*
>
> *(b) two offences are of the same category as each other if they belong to the same category of offences prescribed for the purposes of this section by an order made by the Secretary of State.*

(5) A category prescribed by an order under subsection (4)(b) must consist of offences of the same type.

(6) Only prosecution evidence is admissible under section 101(1)(d).

(7) Where—

> *(a) a defendant has been convicted of an offence under the law of any country outside England and Wales ('the previous offence'), and*
>
> *(b) the previous offence would constitute an offence under the law of England and Wales ('the corresponding offence') if it were done in England and Wales at the time of the trial for the offence with which the defendant is now charged ('the current offence'),*

subsection (8) applies for the purpose of determining if the previous offence and the current offence are of the same description or category.

(8) For the purposes of subsection (2)—

> *(a) the previous offence is of the same description as the current offence if the corresponding offence is of that same description, as set out in subsection (4)(a);*

(b) the previous offence is of the same category as the current offence if the current offence and the corresponding offence belong to the same category of offences prescribed as mentioned in subsection (4)(b)."

[Sub-sections (9), (10) and (11) concern foreign service offences]

4.4.1 The Elements Of Gateway (d)

It can help to approach gateway (d) by breaking down the elements as follows:

1. Identify what kind of bad character evidence it is (i.e. conviction, allegation etc, see Chapter 2.1 and 2.2).

2. Identify an important matter in issue between D and P (see below).

3. Identify how the bad character evidence is relevant to that matter in issue (see Chapter 2.8).

4. Identify any exclusions (see Chapter 5).

4.4.2 How To Use Gateway (d)

The prosecution should not routinely make applications to adduce bad character evidence.[32] A prosecution decision to use bad character evidence should be made on the basis of its usefulness in the case, not because the defendant has or may have a bad character.

Gateway (d) is frequently used for evidence that is relied upon to show a propensity. Propensity is not, however, the only reason for using gateway (d): see the full discussion of possible "*matters in issue*" below.

For situations where gateway (d) and s.103(1)(a) are invoked, the three questions in *Hanson* essentially present, in a different way, the

[32] *Hanson* [2005] EWCA Crim 824, [2005] 2 Cr App R 21, [4].

requirements of, specifically, s.103(1)(a), s.103(2), s.103(3) and s.101(3). These three questions are:[33]

> 1. Does the history of conviction(s) establish a propensity to commit offences of the kind charged?
>
> 2. Does that propensity make it more likely that the defendant committed the offence charged?
>
> 3. Is it unjust to rely on the conviction(s) of the same description or category; and, in any event, will the proceedings be unfair if they are admitted?

The *Hanson* questions are not a substitute for following the full requirements of gateway (d).

Crucially, the questions do not include the gateway requirement of relevance to an important matter in issue.

Further, the questions do not cover all the possibilities that s.103(1)(a) invites: s.103(2) "*is not exhaustive of the types of conviction which might be relied upon to show evidence of propensity to commit offences of the kind charged*", nor does merely having a conviction that is of the same description or category automatically show propensity.[34]

The third question cannot limit the application of s.101(3)[35] to the use of convictions of the same description or category. Clearly s.101(3) applies to all forms of bad character evidence (convictions of any category or otherwise, and non-conviction evidence).

---

33 *Hanson* [2005] EWCA Crim 824, [2005] 2 Cr App R 21, [7].

34 *Hanson* [2005] EWCA Crim 824, [2005] 2 Cr App R 21, [8].

35 As opposed to s.103(3).

Hanson then goes on to make a number of well-known statements about the nature of convictions that are capable of proving propensity in the s.103(1)(a) context.

In brief, these are:

i) Striking similarity is not needed[36] (but a degree of similarity is[37]).

ii) Any number of events may demonstrate a propensity, but in general, fewer convictions provide weaker evidence of propensity. A single conviction of sufficient distinctiveness may in some circumstances be sufficient.[38]

iii) Both s.101(3) and s.103(3) should be considered. Section 101(3) can be influenced by the degree of similarity between

---

36 *Hanson* [2005] EWCA Crim 824, [2005] 2 Cr App R 21, [9]; *Jackson* [2011] EWCA Crim 1870, [32]; *Dossett* [2013] EWCA Crim 710, [28]. Although a few cases, e.g. *Brisland* [2008] EWCA Crim 2773, [13], have still referred to it.

37 *Hassan* [2007] EWCA Crim 1287, [26]; *Jackson* [2011] EWCA Crim 1870, [34] refers to "*circumstances … sufficiently similar to bring probative significance to the previous conviction*".

38 *Hanson* [2005] EWCA Crim 824, [2005] 2 Cr App R 21, [9]. For single conviction not sufficient see *Khan* [2020] EWCA Crim 163; *McGarvie* [2011] EWCA Crim 1414; *Benabbou* [2012] EWCA Crim 1256; *O'Dowd* [2009] EWCA Crim 905, [2009] 2 Cr App R 16. For examples of sufficient single convictions: *Day* [2019] EWCA Crim 935; *Spottiswood* [2019] EWCA Crim 949; *Hay* [2017] EWCA Crim 1851; *Larkin* [2016] EWCA Crim 170; *Brown* [2012] EWCA Crim 773.

the previous conviction and the offence charge. Section 103(3) can be influenced by the strength of the prosecution case.[39]

iv) Old convictions are generally of less assistance and, if used, are more likely to result in unfairness.[40]

v) Propensity to untruthfulness is not the same as propensity to dishonesty. Convictions assist on s.103(1)(b) only if they show untruthfulness in some way and truthfulness is in issue.[41]

vi) Bad character evidence (not just conviction-evidence) cannot be used to bolster a weak case or prejudice the jury against the defendant.[42] As to this see more below.

vii) Parties need to co-operate in establishing the facts of previous convictions, and in some cases more detailed facts will be needed.[43]

---

39 *Hanson* [2005] EWCA Crim 824, [2005] 2 Cr App R 21, [10]; see also *De Vos* [2006] EWCA Crim 1688; *DPP v Chand* [2007] EWHC 90 (Admin); *Thomas* [2010] EWCA Crim 148.

40 *Hanson* [2005] EWCA Crim 824, [2005] 2 Cr App R 21, [11]; *Murphy* [2006] EWCA Crim 3408.

41 *Hanson* [2005] EWCA Crim 824, [2005] 2 Cr App R 21, [13]. See also *Purcell* [2006] EWCA Crim 1264; *Burns* [2006] EWCA Crim 617; *Campbell* [2007] EWCA Crim 1472, [2007] 2 Cr App R 28; *Edwards* [2005] EWCA Crim 1813, [2006] 1 Cr App R 3; *Alobaydi* [2007] EWCA Crim 145; *Garnham* [2008] EWCA Crim 266; cf *Stephenson* [2006] EWCA Crim 2325 (non-defendant); *Clarke* [2011] EWCA Crim 939 (gateway (g)).

42 *Hanson* [2005] EWCA Crim 824, [2005] 2 Cr App R 21, [18].

43 *Hanson* [2005] EWCA Crim 824, [2005] 2 Cr App R 21, [17]; *Steen* [2007] EWCA Crim 335, [2008] 2 Cr App R 26. When bad character evidence is in the form of a conviction, there are sometimes problems in proving the fact of conviction or the facts underlying the conviction. This

viii) The Court of Appeal will only interfere with a judge's decision on bad character evidence in quite limited circumstances.[44]

Hanson is not limited to the use of bad character evidence in the form of convictions used only to show propensity to commit a type of offence. It also covers s.103(1)(b).

The judgment indicates that the observations in relation to s.103(1)(a) can be used in other contexts as well.[45]

Further, it makes a number of statements (about notice, jury warnings, establishing facts, satellite litigation) that are of use in relation to any consideration of s.101 evidence.

4.4.2.1 Satellite litigation

Satellite litigation should be avoided. It consists of the risk that the tribunal of fact will be tempted to 'try' the bad character allegation in an attempt to ascertain its appropriate role in the main question of guilt. Doing so can result in a 'satellite trial' of the bad character allegation, which the Court has cautioned against.[46] Moreover, the current trial is not intended to try the guilt of the defendant in other matters, and the

---

rarely seems to be an obstacle to their ultimate admissibility. For usage of s.74(3) PACE see *C* [2010] EWCA Crim 2971, [2011] 1 WLR 1942.

44 *Hanson* [2005] EWCA Crim 824, [2005] 2 Cr App R 21, [15]; see e.g. *Edwards and Rowlands* [2005] EWCA Crim 3244, [2006] 2 Cr App R 4, also *Renda* [2005] EWCA Crim 2826, [2006] 1 Cr App R 24, where one of the limits on interference is deference to the judge's "*feel*" for the case.

45 As, e.g., *Hanson* [2005] EWCA Crim 824, [2005] 2 Cr App R 21, [13] about the number of convictions in relation to both s.103(1)(a) and (b).

46 See also *Bovell and Dowds* [2005] EWCA Crim 1091, [2005] 2 Cr App R 27; *M* [2006] EWCA Crim 1509; *O'Dowd* [2009] EWCA Crim 905, [2009] 2 Cr App R 16; *Dalby* [2012] EWCA Crim 701, [25].

full evidence necessary for a fair trial of those matters is usually unavailable.

The Court in *McKenzie* adopts several useful principles from *Hanson*:

> *"A single previous conviction is unlikely to show propensity unless it shows a tendency to unusual behaviour or where the particular circumstances demonstrate probative force in relation to the offence charged. The same comments apply to allegations of past misconduct, but here a dilemma arises. If the allegations of previous misconduct are few in number, they may well fail to show propensity even if they are true, but the greater the plethora of collateral allegations, the greater the risk of the trial losing its proper focus."*[47]

An example of sufficiently unusual behaviour is contained in *Spottiswood*: a previous conviction from seven years earlier, where the defendant used a headlock in a particular way, was "*highly distinctive behaviour when carrying out an attack*".[48]

4.4.2.2 Bolstering a weak case

Hanson expressed the principle thus: "*Evidence of bad character cannot be used simply to bolster a weak case, or to prejudice the minds of a jury against a defendant.*" The idea is that the prosecution should not take unfair advantage of a defendant's bad character to plug gaps in the integrity of its case.

While *Hanson* does not expressly say that bad character evidence is *inadmissible* if the prosecution case is weak, the practical effect is that if a case

---

47 *McKenzie* [2008] EWCA Crim 758, [24]; but see the failure to deal with the complication of satellite issues in *Gumbrell* [2009] EWCA Crim 550, [23].

48 *Spottiswood* [2019] EWCA Crim 949, [32]. See also *Bryon* [2015] EWCA Crim 997, involving an unusual method of commercial burglary.

is weak, there is no permissible use the jury can make of the bad character evidence. It is therefore for most practical purposes inadmissible. In some limited cases it may be logical to admit the evidence but direct the jury that if they consider the prosecution case is otherwise weak, they cannot rely on the bad character evidence. This would be an enhanced version of the standard direction that "*D's previous convictions may only be used as some support for the prosecution case. You must not convict D wholly or mainly because of them.*"

There are few cases explicitly applying this principle with success. The weakness or otherwise of the prosecution case is generally one for the reasonable exercise of the judge's discretion.[49]

The Court of Appeal has tended to equate the strength of the prosecution case with whether there is any separate plausible evidence linking the defendant to the crime. It is often akin to the 'no case to answer' criteria:

> "*We note that—realistically—the defence made no submission to the judge that there was no case to answer. That is not, of course, conclusive but we consider that it reflects the fact that the case against the defendant, although partly circumstantial, was well above the Plimsoll line of a weak case below which previous convictions should not be admitted.*"[50]

In *Killick*, the judge rightly excluded evidence under s.101(3) because the prosecution used it to bolster a weak case (that D had committed a commercial burglary). The judge correctly went on to allow submission of no case to answer. The bad character evidence consisted of statements made in interview to the effect that D was a drug user who had a drug debt. The prosecution case depended upon D's DNA being found on a

49 *Powell* [2015] EWCA Crim 2200, [14]; *LN* [2014] EWCA Crim 506; *McDonald* [2007] EWCA Crim 1194.

50 *Stanley* [2016] EWCA Crim 1801, [15]. See also *Richards* [2018] EWCA Crim 2374, [91].

moveable item at the scene of the burglary. The prosecution's reliance on D's partner, whose evidence now provided a possible alibi, left the prosecution in an "*inconsistent position*".[51]

Another successful case is *K*, where the wrongful admission of hearsay evidence meant that the subsequent admission of bad character evidence was actually made against the background of a weak prosecution case.[52] This is an unusual concatenation of circumstances.

In *DPP v Chand*, the judge concluded that the bad character evidence was admissible under gateway (d), but excluded it under s.101(3) because the prosecution case was not strong.[53]

In *Hamidi*, the Court did express concern that the judge's direction had suggested that the jury might, but for the bad character evidence, regard the prosecution case against the defendant as "*unconvincing*". It could be said that the judge was inviting the jury to treat the evidence as sufficient to bolster a weak case.

> *"We have been troubled by this submission. We recognise that the terms in which the Judge expressed himself were capable of giving that impression to the jury. We have to consider whether the jury may reasonably have so understood him. … In these circumstances, we do not consider that the jury could have misunderstood the Judge's intention, namely to point out that if they found that the appellant had participated knowledgably [in the bad character allegation] that was capable of being important evidence going to the issue of knowledge during his participation in the [current charge]. The Judge was not saying and could not reasonably be understood as saying that previous*

51 *Killick* [2020] EWCA Crim 785.

52 *K* [2012] EWCA Crim 2943.

53 *DPP v Chand* [2007] EWHC 90 (Admin).

> *participation in [the earlier alleged fraud] was conclusive. The jury had been specifically directed to the contrary."*[54]

It can be useful to defer the decision on the weakness or strength of the prosecution case until the evidence has been heard, especially in cases relying on circumstantial evidence.[55]

4.4.3 *What Is Propensity?*

The Court of Appeal has regularly examined what "*propensity*" means. There is no unified result. There are countless examples of what propensity means in the context of specific cases. These are of limited use unless one comes across a case that is sufficiently similar to the current case.

As far as useful guiding principles for daily application go, the following may assist.

- Apply *Hanson* above as to propensity and s.103(1).
- Propensity is, at most, an incidental issue. The most important evidence is that which bears directly on the defendant's guilt or innocence. Propensity cannot alone establish guilt and it must not be regarded as a satisfactory substitute for direct evidence of the accused's involvement in the crime charged.[56]
- Excessive recourse to cumulative past incidents may skew the trial in a way which distracts attention from the central issue. This is so even if the past incidents are undoubtedly helpful.[57]

---

54 *Hamidi* [2010] EWCA Crim 66, [38].

55 *Lewis* [2014] EWCA Crim 48, [2014] 2 Cr App R (S) 27, [115]-[117].

56 *Mitchell* [2016] UKSC 55, [2017] AC 571, [55].

57 *Mitchell* [2016] UKSC 55, [2017] AC 571, [53].

- An adverse effect can arise through the sheer weight of disputed evidence on other uncharged allegations.[58] In such cases s.101(3) should be employed.

- Minimise terminology that is not in the legislation or pre-dates the legislation. This includes 'striking similarity', 'similar fact' and 'tendency'.[59]

- Propensity is not "*disposition*" —this means something different in the CJA.[60] Looking for "*disposition*" is largely unhelpful.

- Convictions are not admissible if they merely show a preparedness to engage in crime of "*vaguely the same kind*" as the current offence. "*There must be a logical basis for concluding that the previous offending shows that the defendant was more likely to be prepared to commit the specific crime in question. Provided such a logical connection can be made, there is no requirement that the previous offending should consist of or include an offence of a strikingly, or even markedly closely, similar nature to the index offence.*"[61]

  In *BEF*, the trial judge had been wrong to find that the defendant's conviction for raping a 27-year-old woman in 2020 established a propensity to rape his stepdaughter between 2010-2013 when she was aged 7-10 years old. Properly weighing the similarities and differences between the two kinds of offending, they

58 *Mitchell* [2016] UKSC 55, [2017] AC 571, [53].

59 In 2012 the Court of Appeal, rather than using the legislative terminology of 'bad character evidence', referred instead to "*the admissibility of what may loosely be called 'similar fact' evidence under section 101(1)(c) and (d) CJA*": *Suleman* [2012] EWCA Crim 1569, [2012] 2 Cr App R 30, [4].

60 See Chapter 2.

61 *Dossett* [2013] EWCA Crim 710, [28].

were so different that the 2020 conviction could not demonstrate a propensity to commit offences of the kind now alleged.[62]

- When "*propensity*" bad character evidence is relied upon, bootstrapping is not allowed. See Chapter 6 on cross-admissibility. Thus, if incident A is relied upon as propensity, the jury must be sure of incident A before being permitted to use it as propensity towards the current charge. The jury cannot use the evidence in its entirety (including that of the current charge) to be satisfied of the truth of incident A, and then use incident A as support for the current charge. This is in contrast to the situation where several instances of "*coincidence*" bad character are relied on to form a propensity. Here, the jury should consider the evidence cumulatively, not separately.[63]

- For the standard of proof to be applied to propensity evidence, see Chapter 6.

Subsections 103(2) and (4) set out specific instances in which propensity might more readily be established. The language is permissive but not mandatory ("*may*"). The usefulness of s.103(2) is in practice extremely limited. It is not an alternative route to admissibility and is not an invitation to admit all convictions of the same category or description regardless of their probative effect. Merely being of the same description or the same category does not automatically make convictions admissible.[64] It simply provides one means by which propensity can be identified. The

62 *BEF* [2023] EWCA Crim 1362. The conviction was quashed and a retrial ordered.

63 *Mitchell* [2016] UKSC 55, [2017] AC 571, [49].

64 *Tully and Wood* [2006] EWCA Crim 2270, [27]-[28].

test of relevance (or "*probative force*"[65]) must still be satisfied for each piece of bad character evidence.

Section 103(2) applies only to convictions. Other items of bad character evidence (including cautions) are not covered by s.103(2). However, this has no practical effect because by the words in parenthesis in s.103(2), propensity can be established by wider means those provided by s.103(2).[66]

The exclusion in s.103(3) is limited to a propensity established via s.103(2).

Subsections 103(7) and (8) are parallel provisions for foreign convictions.

Under s.103(4)(a), offences are of the same description as each other if the statement of the offence in a written charge or indictment would, in each case, be in the same terms. This is fairly self-explanatory. In practice, it is largely made up of offences that fall under the same statutory provision.

Under s.103(4)(b), offences fall within the same category as each other if they are so specified in an order made by the Secretary of State. However, by s.103(5), an order can only group together offences that are "*of the same type*". To date, only one such order has been made: the Criminal Justice Act 2003 (Categories of Offences) Order 2004/3346, which came into effect shortly after the bad character statutory provisions in 2004. It specifies a category of 11 theft-related offences, and a category of 36 sexual offences with a person under the age of 16.[67] The Order is rarely

[65] *Tully and Wood* [2006] EWCA Crim 2270, [27].

[66] E.g. *Valencia* [2015] EWCA Crim 857, [17].

[67] Schedule, Part 2 para 25 of the Order was updated on 28 March 2023 to include an offence under s.14 of the Sexual Offences Act 2003 where it involves the commission of an offence under ss.5-8 (ss.9-10 already having been specified in the original version of para 25).

relied upon, as in practice the required propensity is usually evident from the nature of the conviction and/or its particulars. Further, even if two offences appear in the same category, a propensity still has to be established to the court's satisfaction.

Where evidence is said to go to an important matter in issue that is *not* a propensity to commit offences of the kind charged, care should be taken to ensure that the distinction is properly made. The potential for misunderstanding is illustrated by *Mukeh Davies*.[68] There, the Court said:

> *"There is a distinction between evidence of a propensity and evidence of past behaviour which makes it more likely that a defendant acted in a particular way on the occasion of the alleged crime, albeit that the distinction may sometimes be a fine one … On the facts, it is a fine distinction in this case; but the prosecution drew the distinction, as they were entitled to do, and did not seek to prove a relevant propensity."*

Identification of the perpetrator is another example of something that looks like, but is not, propensity. In *Watson*, the matter in issue was the identity of the killer. The Court agreed that bad character evidence

> "*was admissible if it could properly be relied upon by the jury as showing that the appellant had a sexual interest in young boys, and/or that within a short time after [the] murder he acted in ways which were similar to unusual actions by the killer … Such evidence was in our view correctly relied on by the prosecution as going to the identification of the appellant as the killer, rather than as evidence of a relevant propensity. We accept that the distinction is … a fine one; but it was nonetheless a correct distinction.*"[69]

68 *Mukeh Davies* [2023] EWCA Crim 845, [34].

69 *Watson* [2023] EWCA Crim 1016, [67].

4.4.4 *Important Matter In Issue*

Per s.112(1), "'*important matter' means a matter of substantial importance in the context of the case as a whole*".

A deceptively simple phrase, the "*important matter in issue*" actually drives a large part of the operation of gateways (d) and (e), and thus is pivotal in the admission of the majority of bad character evidence that passes through s.101.

4.4.4.1 *The Qualifier Of 'Importance'*

The word "*important*" is used in gateways (d) and (e) (and also in gateway (c) but not in the context of "*matter in issue*").

In the context of "*matter in issue*" for gateways (d) and (e), 112(1) explains to some extent what "*important matter*" means: a matter of substantial importance in the context of the case as a whole where that matter is in issue between the defendant and prosecution, or between two co-defendants. As a definition it is primarily self-defining. The legislation does not say what "*important*", "*substantial importance*", or "*matter*" mean.

As a matter of statutory construction, "*important*" must have a meaning beyond mere relevance which is already a requirement in s.101(1)(d).[70] On a plain reading, "*important*" means that the issue must not be a peripheral or trivial one. The requirement for importance is sometimes omitted.[71]

---

70 See *Watters* [2007] EWCA Crim 1184, [18], citing *Archbold.*

71 *Anderson* [2008] EWCA Crim 837, [11]; *Purcell* [2007] EWCA Crim 2604, [25]; *Saint* [2010] EWCA Crim 1924, [20] (where it might be said the matter in issue was not sufficiently important).

"*Important*" is also designed to keep the fact-finder's attention focused upon those matters that genuinely need to be decided in the case. For example, where bad character evidence is adduced not by way of conviction but by unproved allegations, the danger of distraction is even greater. This has "*the dangers not only of adding to the length and cost of the trial, but of complicating the issues which the jury has to decide and taking the focus away from the most important issue or issues.*"[72]

Campbell emphasises "*importance*" in relation to the specific matter in issue in s.103(1)(b):

> "*The only circumstance in which there is likely to be an important issue as to whether a defendant has a propensity to tell lies is where telling lies is an element of the offence charged. Even then, the propensity to tell lies is only likely to be significant if the lying is in the context of committing criminal offences, in which case the evidence is likely to be admissible under s.103(1)(a).*"[73]

While the interpretation in *Campbell* is restrictive, there is some support for it in subsequent case law: bad character will not automatically assist in determining truthfulness without something more. In particular, although the Court in *LH* states (perhaps a little unforgivingly) that "*[a]ny conviction for a criminal offence is likely to reflect on the credibility of the defendant*", it then goes on to say that "*[o]ld or isolated instances of untruthfulness are generally not likely to be of significant probative value on credibility.*" The fact that the Court focuses on instances of untruthfulness (as opposed to "*any conviction for a criminal offence*") suggests that *Campbell* is not far off the mark when it says that a defendant's credibility

72 *McKenzie* [2008] EWCA Crim 758, [23].

73 *Campbell* [2007] EWCA Crim 1472, [2007] 2 Cr App R 28, [31].

is only assisted by bad character where that bad character specifically shows a propensity to tell lies.[74]

Some guidance on "*substantial*" comes from the gateway (e) context in *Apabhai*, quoting from *Scott*: "*the word substantial must mean that the evidence concerned has something more than trivial probative value*".[75] Thus the court is looking for a significant, substantial, non-trivial matter in issue.

4.4.4.2 Matter In Issue

The CJA does not provide a definition of "*matter in issue*",[76] nor does it contrast it with 'fact in issue'.

A "*matter in issue*" can be framed at any level of abstraction. At the broadest level, the question 'whether the defendant is guilty' is a "*matter in*

[74] The Court also said, "*We do not accept that a single incident where a defendant pleaded not guilty to an offence in respect of which he was subsequently convicted and gave an account which must have been rejected necessarily establishes a propensity for untruthfulness. In this case there were three other convictions in which the applicant had pleaded guilty. It was necessary to stand back and take those into account in determining whether the propensity was established*": *LH* [2017] NICA 67, [23]. See also *O'Sullivan* [2013] EWCA Crim 43.

[75] *Apabhai* [2011] EWCA Crim 917, [42] and *Scott* [2009] EWCA Crim 2457, [45].

[76] The phrase seems to have appeared first, in this context, in the Law Commission Report. It may have been adopted from the CLRC: *Evidence of Bad Character in Criminal Proceedings* (Law Com No 273, 2001), [11.8], quoting the CLRC Bill which uses the phrase. Although the Report refers to case law in sentences containing the phrase, it would appear that these cases have not actually employed that exact phrase. In the pre-CJA case of *Boardman v DPP* [1974] AC 421, their Lordships confine themselves to "*fact in question*": at 442.

issue". So framed, it encompasses the myriad of different factual elements going to the question of guilt or innocence. Equally, the question whether the defendant has some kind of propensity might be a matter in issue. And at the narrow end of the spectrum is a specific factual dispute that needs resolving.

How the legislation intends the phrase to be used is unclear. It may be assumed that it was intended to be used as the Law Commission used it (although this does not necessarily aid clarity), but since there is no definition the phrase has tended to be used in whatever way seems appropriate in the context. In *Darnley* the Court used "*important matter in issue*" to mean: "*important evidence relating to an* issue in dispute *between the prosecution and the defence, within the meaning of gateway (d)*".[77] This interpretation treats 'issue' as the thing in dispute, not 'matter' as the thing in *issue*.

The statutory guidance can be summarised as follows:

- From the two examples given (in s.103(1), and by implication in s.104(1)), a "*matter in issue*" can be a "*question whether the defendant has a propensity*" of two types. However, it is not limited to such a question.

- There are exceptions to the statutory assumption that a defendant's bad character is of probative value in determining guilt. This is what is meant by the concluding phrase of each of s.103(1)(a) and (b). The question whether the defendant has a propensity can have no probative value and can therefore be properly irrelevant (as opposed to being merely inadmissible).

Common matters in issue include:

[77] *Darnley* [2012] EWCA Crim 1148, [31] (emphasis added).

- The elements of the offence charged, unless they are admitted by the defence.[78]

- The defendant's propensity, either to commit offences of the kind charged or to be untruthful. These are created matters in issue by virtue of s.103(1) and s.104(1). Note that s.103(1)(b) is limited in application. The question of the defendant's propensity to be untruthful will normally only be capable of being described as an important matter in issue "*where telling lies is an element of the offence charged.*"[79]

- The "*genesis of the complaint*".[80] In *M*, the circumstances in which C's allegations came to light were important; thus, the jury could be told that C made allegations when encouraged to do so by K, who also made similar allegations against D and later withdrew them.

- The defendant's state of mind[81] or intention. In *Lanning*, "*the contention that a stabbing was not deliberate and instead the deceased turned onto the knife can equally be an important " matter in*

---

[78] In *Swellings* [2009] EWCA Crim 3249, [2009] 2 Cr App R (S) 30, D admitted manslaughter and admitted he had struck one blow, but said he then distanced himself from what followed. This meant that he did not accept he had been part of a joint enterprise after that point. This physical act was still in dispute and so his propensity to street violence in a gang was relevant. The important matter in issue was this propensity.

[79] *Campbell* [2007] EWCA Crim 1472, [2007] 2 Cr App R 28, [15]. But note that *Highton* provides a way around this: see gateway (g) below.

[80] *M* [2009] EWCA Crim 2504, [10]. The Court of Appeal did not object to that statement; it overruled the decision to use gateway (d) only because the evidence was not of bad character within the meaning of s.112(1).

[81] *Brand* [2009] EWCA Crim 2878.

> *issue ", ... relevant and probative evidence can potentially be called to rebut the suggestion that the fatality was an accident.*"[82]

"*Matters in issue*" do not include:

- Facts which have been agreed by the parties.[83] Thus, if the defendant accepts that he drove dangerously, convictions showing that he had driven dangerously on other occasions are not admissible for the purpose of establishing a propensity to do so.[84]

- Facts which do not assist the tribunal of fact to reach a verdict.[85]

- Points that merely arise in the course of the investigation/trial and are not necessary for its resolution.

Therefore, evidence that has (or may have) relevance only to these types of facts is inadmissible.

---

82 See *Lanning* [2021] EWCA Crim 450, [51].

83 All might agree that C's watch was found in a pawn shop. P does not need to prove that the watch found in the shop belongs to C, and D does not need to attempt to rebut it. Evidence that is relevant to that fact is therefore inadmissible for the purpose of proving that it is true.

84 *Phair* [2022] NICA 66, [44]. In *Goddard* [2012] EWCA Crim 1756, it was wrong to admit convictions for possessing indecent images of children in a trial for conspiracy to rape a young boy, because both defendants had already admitted they had a sexual interest in young boys. These highly prejudicial convictions were therefore irrelevant to any matters in issue at the trial.

85 For example, if the defendant is charged with an offence of strict liability, his assertion that he did not intend to commit the act would not affect the verdict (although it may affect sentence).

Problems commonly arise where (1) a peripheral matter is treated as an important matter, or where the matter is not actually in issue,[86] and (2) where inadequate reasoning is given for the identification of a matter in issue.

See *Saint*, discussed in the context of gateway (c) above. The defendant was convicted (in 2009) of false imprisonment, two indecent assaults, and rape against C, occurring in a car park in 1989. The judge had wrongly admitted bad character evidence via gateway (c) to the effect that in the mid-1990s the defendant visited the car park at night.

In respect of gateway (d), propensity could not be the matter in issue, but there was another possibility because "*the Crown had a legitimate interest in proving that the appellant was in the habit of frequenting the car park and the surrounding area late at night.*"[87] However, as the Court said, this is only an *interest*, not a matter in issue: the case could be proved without showing the habit. In fact, evidence showing that the defendant simply had this habit is by itself not even bad character evidence, although in this case there were bad character aspects as well, mainly those that alleged non-consensually watching other people having sexual intercourse.

The prosecution also suggested that the evidence could help to establish the identity of the person whose footsteps had been heard prior to the assault. The prosecution was better able to prove that identity if it could adduce evidence not just of the defendant's habit of frequenting the area late at night but also of his interest in watching people having sex.[88] The

---

86 E.g. in *Mustapha* [2007] EWCA Crim 1702, [13], the judge said the "*important question*" was whether the defendant had a propensity to possess firearms and live ammunition. The Court of Appeal agreed that this was an incorrect use of s.103(1)(a), because the present offence was not about firearm possession.

87 *Saint* [2010] EWCA Crim 1924, [19].

88 The footsteps were heard just after the complainant had had consensual sexual intercourse in her car with another man.

Court of Appeal said this was unlikely to constitute an important matter in issue. *"[R]ealistically and in the light of all the other evidence in the case, the footsteps issue was probably not of 'substantial importance' and did not justify the admission of the bad character evidence under gateway (d)."*[89] The evidence having been wrongly admitted under both gateways (c) and (d), the conviction was unsafe.

In *Urushadze* the question was whether the defendant was part of a joint enterprise to rob the victim, or whether he had not witnessed the first part of the incident and was only trying to defend an acquaintance against people apparently attacking him. the defendant had previous convictions for shoplifting which were admitted under gateway (d). It was said that the convictions were relevant to the matter in issue of the defendant's propensity "*to know and perceive that a theft was taking place—a theft with violence, hence a robbery*".[90]

The Court of Appeal said the evidence should not have been admitted under any circumstances, because the propensity to know that a theft is taking place (if such a thing exists) was not capable of being established by the convictions. Moreover, the present charge was for violent theft whereas the convictions were for shoplifting, unlikely to cast any light on how the defendant perceived the present events or to establish a propensity to commit robbery of the type in question. Even if it did have limited probative value, this was "*very greatly outweighed*" by the prejudice caused; s.101(3) should have been applied.[91]

In *Bello*, D1 t was accused of fraudulently passing on customers' credit cards to D2. The bad character evidence suggested that D1 had six months earlier fraudulently used a customer's credit card to transfer

---

89 *Saint* [2010] EWCA Crim 1924, [20]. It was not relevant that the defendant was also involved in consensual promiscuity at the time: at [19]. This would be to mistake prejudice for relevance.

90 *Urushadze* [2008] EWCA Crim 2498, [21].

91 *Urushadze* [2008] EWCA Crim 2498, [28].

money to a friend's credit card. In D1's home was a piece of paper containing a credit card number and expiry date. They matched those of a credit card that had been issued to D1's friend, allegedly fraudulently, in the uncharged set of events. The judge said: "*I have no doubt … that this [piece of paper] was relevant under section 101(1)(d) … to an important matter in issue between the defendant and the prosecution, which is* whether the defendant has committed this offence." [92]

This approach widens the "*matter in issue*" as far as it can possibly go, making the 'matter' equivalent to the defendant's 'guilt'. This approach illustrates the opposite extreme to the 'peripheral matters problem' raised above. It holds that "*an important matter in issue*" can be applied so broadly as to encompass the actual question of the defendant's guilt—which is the occupation of any trial on a plea of not guilty. It does not need to be a specific matter.

Caution is needed to avoid the eventuality *Hanson* warned against in the context of gateway (d): the prosecution making routine applications to admit bad character evidence without regard to the circumstances of each case.[93]

4.4.5 Gang Evidence and Gateway (d)

Evidence showing that a defendant is a member of, or associated with, street/criminal gangs in a relevant area can be gateway (d) evidence.

This approach is not always easy to reconcile with the law on guilt by association. In *Kane*, the Court of Appeal strongly criticised the use of bad character evidence to show "*guilt by association*". There, the defendant's close involvement or association with others having extensive criminal convictions was inadmissible at his trial for blackmail:

---

[92] *Bello* [2007] EWCA Crim 2499, [8] (emphasis added).

[93] *Hanson* [2005] EWCA Crim 824, [2005] 2 Cr App R 21, [4].

> *"The propensity is not to be equated with some kind of propensity to commit offences generally. [The prosecution] has been more or less explicit in saying that really why the prosecution wanted this evidence in was that they indeed wanted the jury to know 'the nature of the man with whom they were dealing.' That cannot possibly in itself be a sufficient justification for admitting the evidence or a sufficient justification for the prosecution even to try and persuade the Crown Court judge to admit that evidence. Guilt by association of itself has never been part of England and Wales criminal law."*[94]

That case was decided in 2013. In 2020, *Hassan* distinguished *Kane*. There, largely uncharged/non-conviction evidence of D's association with drugs and drug dealers was admissible under gateway (d) as going to the motive for D committing murder.[95] The trend of recent case law is clear: a judge may admit evidence that D is associated with a gang.

4.4.5.1 Is Gang Evidence Bad Character Evidence?

The most often encountered view is that membership or association generally involves, prima facie, "*implications of bad behaviour*".[96] In *Abdi*, the defendant was convicted of the murder of J in November 2018. He had himself been the victim of two shootings, one in August 2018 and another, after J's murder, in February 2019. The prosecution case was that the first showed a motive to commit the murder and the second showed a revenge attack by the rival gang. The Court held that this was bad

---

94 *Kane* [2013] EWCA Crim 1487, [29]-[30].

95 *Hassan* [2020] EWCA Crim 761, [15].

96 *Myers (Bermuda)* [2015] UKPC 40, [2016] AC 314, [42]. Note that although *Myers* is concerned with a different test for admissibility (not the CJA 2003), the Privy Council's guidance concerning other matters (police officers as experts, and what might constitute relevant gang evidence) is applicable to cases under the CJA 2003 (see *Abdi* [2022] EWCA Crim 315).

character evidence, correctly admitted via s.98(a).[97] It was relevant that the defendant did not make any complaint or assist the police to investigate the two attacks on him.

For a contrary view, see *Rowe*, where the fact that J had been a victim of gang-related crime was not considered to be bad character evidence. The evidence was

> "*intended to show that [D] would have been aware of the potential danger of standing around the shrine of [a deceased rival gang member]. This was not bad character evidence and had it been thought that this evidence would lead to an unsafe conviction, application to discharge the jury should have been made at the time.*"

In general, it is likely to be more appropriate to treat gang evidence as bad character evidence. The statutory protections are then available to counter prejudice and assumptions and restrict any unfair usage by a jury.

It is common to approach admissibility via both s.98(a) and gateway (d) evidence.[98] Gang evidence is often s.98(a) evidence, as in *Heslop*: "*What otherwise might have been viewed as a random or inexplicable shooting, was on the prosecution's case a vital event forming part of the ongoing feud between two drug gangs*".[99]

4.4.5.2 Admissibility Of Gang Evidence

The test for admitting gang evidence is set out in *Lewis*, although note that it does not cover all eventualities:

97 *Abdi* [2022] EWCA Crim 315, [31]-[33].

98 *Rashid* [2019] EWCA Crim 2018, [36]-[37].

99 *Heslop* [2022] EWCA Crim 897, [49].

"Analysing the issue in a case such as the present, there are four questions that a judge has to consider:

(1) Is the evidence relevant to an important matter in issue between a defendant and the prosecution?

(2) Is there proper evidence of the existence and nature of the gang or gangs?

(3) Does the evidence, if accepted, go to show the defendant was a member of or associated with a gang or gangs which exhibited violence or hostility to the police or with links with firearms?

(4) If the evidence is admitted, will it have such an adverse effect on the fairness of the proceedings that it ought to be excluded?"[100]

"*Proper evidence*" for the purposes of question (2) usually consists of a combination of the following types of evidence, all of which can be admissible depending on the case:

- Expert police evidence based on accumulated knowledge and experience: see *Myers* below.
- Membership and activities of gangs in a particular area
- Evidence of motive[101] and evidence of a shared motive.[102] It is not a precondition for the introduction of gang evidence that the prosecution is able to establish that there had been a "*trigger*

---

[100] *Lewis* [2014] EWCA Crim 48, [2014] 2 Cr App R (S) 27, [82].

[101] *Abdi* [2022] EWCA Crim 315. Motive is often not an element of the offending, but it is generally relevant evidence if it exists.

[102] *Myers (Bermuda)* [2015] UKPC 40, [2016] AC 314, [45].

event".[103] It may suffice to describe a motive by reference to a long-running gang feud.[104]

- The meaning of language, including song lyrics, said to be used by them.
- Videos and similar material showing association with others
- Commonalities between weapons used by other members of a gang and those said to be used in the present case[105]

Evidence that is not usually "*proper evidence*" for the purposes of (2) includes evidence of general illegal activity, e.g. drug dealing or money laundering, by a gang. This is not relevant evidence without more.[106]

Gang evidence can be admissible bad character evidence even where there is no indication that the alleged offending was gang-related. In *Williams*, although "*there was no evidence of the shooting here being gang related*", the Court of Appeal said that the gang evidence was relevant to an important matter in issue under gateway (d), namely "*whether the applicant had been correctly identified as present at the shooting. The evidence going to [the gang] and his association with [the gang] was clearly relevant to that issue.*"[107]

Lyrics and videos: the defendant's appearance in YouTube music videos alongside members of a specific gang can be used to conclude that the defendant is a member of that gang. This is capable of being bad character

---

103 *Heslop* [2022] EWCA Crim 897, [44].

104 *Dixon-Kenton* [2021] EWCA Crim 673, [36].

105 *Myers (Bermuda)* [2015] UKPC 40, [2016] AC 314, [48]

106 *Myers (Bermuda)* [2015] UKPC 40, [2016] AC 314, [72]; *Bernard-Sewell* [2022] EWCA Crim 197, [15].

107 *Williams* [2024] EWCA Crim 1188, [11].

evidence.[108] In *Abdi* an expert gave evidence that particular lyrics in a video referred to stabbing someone.[109] In *Dibba*, lyrics in a drill video that described an escalation from stabbing to shooting were admissible bad character evidence.[110]

In *Okokono*, discussed above in relation to gateway (c), one of the three ways in which bad character evidence was said to be admissible was under gateway (d): to establish the defendant's willingness to engage in gang fights, knowing that others had a propensity to use knives to lethal effect.[111] One difficulty with this reasoning is that the defendant's conviction was only for possession of a knife. There was no evidence that he had engaged in a fight at the time of that conviction.

In another gang-related case, *Mullings*, D was convicted of possessing a firearm with intent to endanger life. He and several other defendants were said to be part of a gang that had confronted a rival gang. The subsequent events led to a murder. D did not himself carry a firearm. The question was whether he was aware that others in the group were carrying firearms with the requisite intent, and participated with that knowledge and with the same intention.[112] He was arrested in March 2007; in November 2007 letters sent to him in prison were found. They included material about the particular gangs, showing allegiances and enmities held by the unknown authors.

---

108 *Abdi* [2022] EWCA Crim 315

109 *Abdi* [2022] EWCA Crim 315

110 *Dibba* [2023] EWCA Crim 576

111 *Okokono* [2014] EWCA Crim 2521, [60]. See also *Awoyemi* [2016] EWCA Crim 668; *Stewart* [2016] EWCA Crim 447; *Lunkulu* [2015] EWCA Crim 1350.

112 *Mullings* [2010] EWCA Crim 2820, [2011] 2 Cr App R 2, [10].

The Court of Appeal held that D's receipt and/or retention of the letters[113] could be used by the jury as evidence of bad character which went to the question whether D participated in a group activity of whose objectives he was aware.[114] It did not matter that the letters were received after the event, or that he had not himself expressed the views contained within the letters. It was admissible under gateway (d) since it went to an important issue in the case.[115] If it was not bad character evidence, it was admissible under the common law as relevant to the issues of joint possession and intention.

It may be asked how letters written by another can be relevant to the defendant's "*disposition*". There are many reasons why he might receive or retain the letters, not necessarily casting light on his own disposition or indicating reprehensible behaviour. The only real relevance is that D's knowledge (now evidenced in the letters) of the behaviour of known gang members may have informed his presence and intention at the scene of the crime earlier in the year. Whether this is true bad character evidence might be open to debate.

4.4.5.3 Expert Evidence On Gangs

Relevant experts are usually, but not always, police officers or people associated with crime and policing.

---

113 *Mullings* [2010] EWCA Crim 2820, [2011] 2 Cr App R 2, [22]: "*the possession and retention of these documents constituted evidence from which the jury could infer that the appellant identified himself with the sentiments they expressed. Had the letters been admitted to prove a disposition towards misconduct the jury would have required a careful direction to the effect that they could not use the letters for this purpose unless they were sure that possession and/or retention of the letters established the appellant's disposition.*"

114 *Mullings* [2010] EWCA Crim 2820, [2011] 2 Cr App R 2, [32].

115 With neither s.78 of PACE nor s.101(3) operating on the facts.

Myers sets out the test for admitting expert police evidence in relation to gangs.

Police officers can be experts, because of their training, experience, and/or knowledge. But, they must then act according to the ordinary rules for experts, which

> *"can be difficult for a police officer who is effectively combining the duties of active investigator (if not of the current case) with those of independent expert. It is particularly important that such a witness should fully understand that once he is tendered as an expert he is not simply a part of the prosecution team, but has a separate duty to the court to give independent evidence, whichever side it may favour. In particular a police expert needs to be especially conscious of the duty to state fully any material which weighs against any proposition which he is advancing, as well as all the evidence on which he has based that proposition. When considering an application by the Crown to adduce the evidence of a police expert, it is incumbent upon the judge to satisfy himself that these duties are recognised, and discharged."*

A police expert must make full disclosure of the nature of their material. Their duty involves at least the following:

(a) Set out their qualifications to give expert evidence, by training and experience.

(b) State not only their conclusions but also how they have arrived at them:

(i) if based on their own observations or contacts with particular persons, the expert must say so;

(ii) if they are based on information provided by other officers the expert must show how it is collected and exchanged and, if recorded, how;

(iii) if they are based on informers, the expert must at least acknowledge that such is one source, although of course they need not name them.

(c) In relation to primary conclusions in relation to D or other key persons, the expert must go beyond a mere general statement that they have sources of kinds A, B and C, but must say whence the particular information they are advancing has come; an example would be observations of D in the company of others known to be members of a gang.

The hearsay rules apply to expert evidence of gang activity. Thus, although an expert may use material assembled by others working in the field, that license does not extend to the assertion of a particular fact in issue in the case. Evidence of the second type is <u>not</u> expert evidence "*even if it may be given by someone who is also an expert*".[116]

4.5 Gateway (e): S.101(1)(e)

"(e) it has substantial probative value in relation to an important matter in issue between the defendant and a co-defendant"

"104 'Matter in issue between the defendant and a co-defendant'

(1) Evidence which is relevant to the question whether the defendant has a propensity to be untruthful is admissible on that basis under section 101(1)(e) only if the nature or conduct of his defence is such as to undermine the co-defendant's defence.

(2) Only evidence—

(a) which is to be (or has been) adduced by the co-defendant, or

116 *Myers (Bermuda)* [2015] UKPC 40, [2016] AC 314, [66].

> *(b) which a witness is to be invited to give (or has given) in cross-examination by the co-defendant,*

is admissible under section 101(1)(e)."

4.5.1 What Is A Co-Defendant?

Section 112(1) provides the following definitions:

"'defendant', in relation to criminal proceedings, means a person charged with an offence in those proceedings;

"'co- defendant', in relation to a defendant, means a person charged with an offence in the same proceedings."

For most practical purposes, this means a person who is charged on the same indictment as D1.

However, a person who was originally a co-defendant (D2) but has, before trial, been dealt with another way (e.g. entered an acceptable plea and awaits sentence pending the conclusion of D1's trial on the same or related charges) is *not* a co-defendant for the purposes of D1's trial:[117]

> "*we consider that [G, who had pleaded guilty] was not a co-defendant within the meaning of section 101(1)(e) which, given the terms of section 104, is only concerned with a co-defendant who is tried in the same proceedings before the same jury, which G was not.*"

Thus, an application to adduce evidence of D2's bad character must be made under s.100, not gateway (e).

[117] *Jukes* [2018] EWCA Crim 176, [32].

If D2 is tried in his absence, he is still a co-defendant and gateway (e) can be used. Of course, D2's absence is likely to mean that there are fewer matters in issue available for D1 to use.[118]

4.5.2 Substantial Probative Value

In theory, this phrase bears the same meaning as in s.100(1)(b).

However, in the context of gateway (e), it bears particular importance (see Chapter 5 on exclusions).

In *Phillips* it was held that, in order to satisfy gateway (e), "*where the defendant is seeking to prove a relevant propensity he must first establish that … the evidence is substantially probative of the propensity* and *that the propensity alleged is substantially probative of the fact in issue.*"[119]

It is correct that evidence of the defendant's bad character must be substantially probative of the important matter in issue (commonly, propensity to commit similar offences or untruthfulness). But the legislation does not require that the propensity be "*substantially probative*" of any 'fact in issue'. It merely needs to be of substantial *importance* in the context of the case as a whole. The propensity itself is the matter in issue, and does not, under the bad character provisions, have to have relevance to any other issue in the case (whether "*matter in issue*" or 'fact in issue'), although of course it may do so.

What is clear from *Phillips* is the reformulation of the meaning of "*substantial probative value*" in the special context of gateway (e).

---

118 *Lee* [2005] EWCA Crim 3459: "*Had [D2] been present to assert more than he had [in a previous interview], a sufficiently important issue might have arisen to have resulted in [D1's] convictions going before the jury, but given [D2's] absence that would not be possible*" at [17].

119 *Phillips* [2011] EWCA Crim 2935, [2012] 1 Cr App R 25, [41] (emphasis in original).

The Court of Appeal rejected the old meaning of "*something more than trivial probative value*", replacing it with the concept of "*an enhanced capability of proving or disproving a matter in issue*".[120] This also applies to the test under s.100(1)(b).[121] It is clear that one effect of this higher standard of admission is to make it harder for a defendant to use another's bad character, under both gateway (e) (in respect of a co-defendant), and s.100(1)(b) (in respect of a prosecution witness).

In case law applying *Phillips*[122] a further embellishment has emerged. The enhanced relevance meaning of "*substantial probative value*" in s.100(1)(b) (and, presumably therefore, s.101(1)(e)) also requires accounting for the threat of satellite litigation. In *Dizaei* the Court of Appeal said, citing *Phillips*, that

> *"If … the judge correctly directs the jury that they must not consider the alleged bad character evidence unless they are sure that it is true, two trials would be simultaneously in progress before the same jury.*
> …
>
> *"In our judgment these are relevant considerations bearing on the assessment of the probative value of the evidence sought to be adduced and its importance in the overall context of the case. When it is assessing the probative value of the evidence in accordance with s.100(1)(b) and s.100(3), and consistently with s.100(2), among the factors relevant to the admissibility judgment, the court should reflect*

120 *Phillips* [2011] EWCA Crim 2935, [2012] 1 Cr App R 25, [39]. This is a higher test than that of "*marginal or trivial value*" in the Explanatory Notes to the CJA, [375].

121 "*[T]he legal meaning of the term 'substantial probative value' must be the same*" for both gateway (e) and s.100(1)(b): *Phillips* [2011] EWCA Crim 2935, [2012] 1 Cr App R 25, [38].

122 *Byrne* [2021] EWCA Crim 107; *Turnbull* [2013] EWCA Crim 676 (gateway (e)); *Walsh* [2012] EWCA Crim 2728; *Sixto* [2012] EWCA Crim 2615; *Dizaei* [2013] EWCA Crim 88, [2013] 1 Cr App R 31.

> *whether the admission of the evidence relating to the bad character of the witness might make it difficult for the jury to understand the remainder of the evidence, and whether its understanding of the case as a whole might be diminished. In such cases the conclusion may be that the evidence is not of substantial probative value ... or that the evidence is not of substantial importance in the context of the case as a whole, or both. If so, the pre-conditions to admissibility will not be established."*[123]

Thus, the assessment of substantial probative value of bad character evidence now includes the risk that the jury might become distracted from its focus on the offence at hand by the admission of that evidence. *Dizaei* treats this as a factor that may be considered under s.100(3); it is, however, somewhat different to the other factors that are listed there, which concern the value of the bad character evidence itself upon the assumption (s.109) that it is true. The focus is not upon proving that the evidence is true, which is the cause of the problem of satellite litigation. It might be argued that such a factor is not relevant[124] to the assessment of probative value.

However, as discussed in Chapter 5 (exclusions), this approach to "*substantial probative value*" is designed partly to counter the lack of any exclusionary provision in respect of gateway (e). Where prosecution evidence is concerned and an exclusionary provision exists (such as s.101(3) or s.78), the risk of satellite litigation falls to be considered when exercising that exclusionary power, not when deciding admissibility under a relevance-based test. The *Phillips* line of reasoning has, in an effort

---

[123] *Dizaei* [2013] EWCA Crim 88, [2013] 1 Cr App R 31, [37]-[38]. Note that s.100(1)(b)(ii) does not actually lead to a conclusion "*that the evidence is not of substantial importance in the context of the case as a whole*". s.100(1)(b)(ii) relates to the "*matter*", not the "*evidence*".

[124] Section 100(3) begins: "*In assessing the probative value of evidence for the purposes of subsection (1)(b) the court must have regard to the following factors (and to any others it considers* <u>relevant</u>*) ...*" (emphasis added).

to provide a substitute-exclusionary power, included such considerations in the test for substantial probative value for defence evidence.[125]

What is the difference between "*relevance*" and "*substantial probative value*"?

Prima facie, relevance is a lower threshold than substantial probative value.

This can be illustrated by the case of *McLean* (*Edwards and Rowlands*), where bad character evidence was inadmissible via gateway (d) but *admissible* via gateway (e).

D1 was convicted of two counts of wounding with intent. He had previous convictions for wounding with intent using a knife in 1998, two offences of battery in 2001, and affray in 2004.

The prosecution's 'application' to admit these via gateway (d), to establish a propensity for violence, was rejected.[126]

However, the judge then admitted the convictions at the behest of D2 under gateway (e). The judge ruled that the important matter in issue between the defendants was created by the separate versions of events that were put forward by each defendant, and that D1's bad character had substantial probative value in relation to that issue. "*[I]f each defendant was saying he was not involved in the violence, and one has previous convictions for violence, that must have substantial probative value on the issue between them.*"[127] It could be said that this looks very similar to the

125 Given its focus on the lack of exclusionary provisions for defence evidence, the Court in *Phillips* probably did not intend to suggest modifications to the existing exclusionary provisions for prosecution evidence.

126 *Edwards and Rowlands* [2005] EWCA Crim 3244, [2006] 2 Cr App R 4, [48].

127 *Edwards and Rowlands* [2005] EWCA Crim 3244, [2006] 2 Cr App R 4, [51].

prosecution's propensity argument: if a defendant has convictions for violent behaviour, this may influence the question whether he has committed the present offence involving violent behaviour.[128]

On appeal, D1 queried why the gateway (e) application succeeded but the less stringent relevance threshold in gateway (d) had failed.

The Court of Appeal said that "*[d]ifferent considerations applied to the co-defendant's application which was made under a different provision, namely s.101(1)(e).*"[129] However, it is also true that there are many *similar* considerations between the two gateways. In particular, the essence of the "*matter in issue*" in both gateway (d) and gateway (e) was based upon the fact that both D1's convictions and the present charge involved violence.

When two gateways have been applied in respect of the same evidence with different outcomes, it should be possible to confirm correct application of the law by identifying which elements of the second gateway have given the different result.

This is especially so when gateways (d) and (e) are concerned, because they are very similar.

- Their points of difference are
  - "*Substantial probative value*" rather than "*relevant*";
  - The parties between whom the matter in issue arises.[130]

---

128 For a case where there was no real difference, see *Khan* [2015] EWCA Crim 1755, [11]-[16].

129 *Edwards and Rowlands* [2005] EWCA Crim 3244, [2006] 2 Cr App R 4, [49].

130 There is also the qualification in s.104(1), which was not applicable in this case, and the exclusions to gateway (d), which were not applied; if they

- The points of similarity are
    - The requirement for a "*matter in issue*";
    - The requirement that it be important;
    - The base requirement of "*relevant*" (because the higher standard in gateway (e) must necessarily satisfy this lower common standard).

Where one piece of evidence is tested against both gateways, then, it is possible to identify (1) whether each gateway concerns the same matter in issue in respect of which the evidence is said to be relevant, (2) whether the matter is important in both gateways as between the respective parties, and (3) whether the evidence is relevant in respect of both gateways.

4.5.3 Matter In Issue Between Defendants

Examples of matters in issue:

- See above possible "*matters in issue*" in relation to gateway (d). These include common matters in issue such as propensity to commit particular kinds of offences or to behave in a particular way.

- Section 104(1) creates an additional matter in issue: propensity to be untruthful is a matter in issue if the nature or conduct of D1's defence is such as to undermine D2's defence. This is narrower than s.103(1)(b). The purpose of showing D1's propensity to be untruthful is usually to influence the jury's belief in his defence, that is, whether or not he committed the offence.[131]

---

were, would only apply after the assessment of the elements of the gateway.

[131] *De Vos* [2006] EWCA Crim 1688, [17].

However, s.104(1) is just one example of a matter in issue. It is not mandatory in all gateway (e) cases.[132]

- A matter in issue between co-defendants can be created or triggered by prosecution actions or tactics.

- A matter in issue between a defendant and the prosecution can also be a matter in issue between co-defendants.

- The credibility of a defendant is a matter in issue for gateway (e) purposes.[133]

In *West*, D was convicted of murder and false imprisonment. His co-defendants, O and B, were both acquitted. D had convictions for dishonesty, and O had numerous convictions, including four counts of actual bodily harm, two s.20 wounding offences, affray, and an assault on the police. There had been no indication of any cut-throat defences. After D gave evidence, and before O was to give evidence, D indicated that he wished to cross-examine O about his previous convictions. The judge refused, on the basis that it would not be possible to ensure fair trial for O, especially as D had already given evidence.[134] However, when the prosecution cross-examined O, O blamed D for the killing, stating that D had "*whacked*" the victim. D again applied to cross-examine O about O's previous convictions. The judge refused, this time because the

132 *Daly* [2014] EWCA Crim 2117, [14]-[15].

133 See *Rosato* [2008] EWCA Crim 1243, [22]: "*In this case there is no dispute that there was an important matter in issue between the appellant and [D2], because the effect of the appellant's evidence was to put the responsibility for the arson onto the shoulders of [D2]. [D2] therefore had an interest in being able to deploy before the jury any material properly relevant in considering whether they should regard this appellant as a credible witness.*"

134 *West* [2006] EWCA Crim 1843, [17].

"*matter in issue was not an issue between [the defendant] and [O] but an issue between [O] and the prosecution*".[135]

Plainly, as the Court of Appeal held, there was undoubtedly an important matter in issue for gateway (e) purposes,[136] even though the situation had been created by an interaction between the prosecution and a co-defendant. O's convictions, and particularly those for violent offences, went to a matter in issue between the defendants, namely who was telling the truth about the violence suffered by the victim.

In a case like *West*, carefully identifying the matter in issue may make it easier to identify which parties might be affected by it.[137]

Obeng sets out the approach where defendants are not facing a joint charge *and* there is no cut-throat defence:

- *"first, what is the fact in issue*[138] *between the defendants;*
- *secondly, is that an important issue between them;*
- *thirdly, does the antecedent character have substantial probative value in resolving that issue; and,*

---

135 *West* [2006] EWCA Crim 1843, [19].

136 *West* [2006] EWCA Crim 1843, [21].

137 In *McAfee* [2006] EWCA Crim 2914 the matter in issue might have been credibility, propensity to commit arson, or whether the defendant had been taking drugs. Given that four gateways were being discussed ((d), (e), (f) and (g)), it may have assisted to identify distinctly the matter in issue for each of (d) and (e). The failure to do so is complicated by the fact that the co-defendant, not the prosecution, made the specific arguments about gateways (f) and (g).

138 Presumably meaning "*matter in issue*".

- *fourthly, does the resolution of that issue assist with the ultimate issue?"*[139]

A matter in issue does not necessarily arise just because defendants give different versions of what happened. *Edwards and Rowlands* states that a mere denial of participation may not give rise to a matter in issue that satisfies gateway (e).[140] Whether it is a mere denial will be a question of fact.[141]

A matter in issue between co-defendants does not arise if it is only in issue between one defendant and the prosecution. Thus in *Woolley* the judge was correct to hold that evidence which "*might prove that [D1] was more involved in the production and supply of cannabis ... did not prove that [D2] was not, or was less likely to be, involved, which was the real issue as between [D2] and [D1].*"[142] The matter to which the bad character evidence was relevant was D1's propensity to engage in drug-related offences, which went to his own guilt. That was a matter for the prosecution. On these particular facts, D1's tendency to engage in drug-related offences did not indicate D2's innocence.

4.6 Gateway (f): S.101(1)(f)

"(f) it is evidence to correct a false impression given by the defendant"

---

139 *Obeng* [2016] EWCA Crim 1797, [32].

140 *Edwards and Rowlands* [2005] EWCA Crim 3244, [2006] 2 Cr App R 4, [1](vi).

141 See *Edwards and Rowlands* [2005] EWCA Crim 3244, [2006] 2 Cr App R 4, [25] where the Court found that Rowlands made more than a mere denial. Also, the case of *McLean* where simply giving "*separate versions of what had occurred*" created an "*important issue*" between the defendants: [51].

142 *Woolley* [2011] EWCA Crim 2758, [15].

"105 'Evidence to correct a false impression'

(1) For the purposes of section 101(1)(f)—

(a) the defendant gives a false impression if he is responsible for the making of an express or implied assertion which is apt to give the court or jury a false or misleading impression about the defendant;

(b) evidence to correct such an impression is evidence which has probative value in correcting it.

(2) A defendant is treated as being responsible for the making of an assertion if—

(a) the assertion is made by the defendant in the proceedings (whether or not in evidence given by him),

(b) the assertion was made by the defendant—

(i) on being questioned under caution, before charge, about the offence with which he is charged, or

(ii) on being charged with the offence or officially informed that he might be prosecuted for it, and evidence of the assertion is given in the proceedings,

(c) the assertion is made by a witness called by the defendant,

(d) the assertion is made by any witness in cross-examination in response to a question asked by the defendant that is intended to elicit it, or is likely to do so, or

(e) the assertion was made by any person out of court, and the defendant adduces evidence of it in the proceedings.

(3) A defendant who would otherwise be treated as responsible for the making of an assertion shall not be so treated if, or to the extent that, he withdraws it or disassociates himself from it.

(4) Where it appears to the court that a defendant, by means of his conduct (other than the giving of evidence) in the proceedings, is seeking to give the court or jury an impression about himself that is false or misleading, the court may if it appears just to do so treat the defendant as being responsible for the making of an assertion which is apt to give that impression.

(5) In subsection (4) 'conduct' includes appearance or dress.

(6) Evidence is admissible under section 101(1)(f) only if it goes no further than is necessary to correct the false impression.

(7) Only prosecution evidence is admissible under section 101(1)(f)."

Gateway (f) is not very commonly employed, nor does it attract a great deal of analysis in the courts. This may be attributed to its comparatively specific threshold requirement which, unlike gateways (c) or (d), cannot readily be expanded to cover a number of associated scenarios.[143] It is quite frequently rejected for failing to apply on the facts.

A defendant must give a false impression about himself, either by express or implied assertion, following which the prosecution may adduce evidence of his bad character only to correct that impression.

143 The Court of Appeal is also rather swift to address such misuses: see, e.g. *Eyidah* [2010] EWCA Crim 987, where no false impression had been identified at all. However contrast *Lewis* [2008] EWCA Crim 424, where it was arguable whether D was giving a false impression about himself; and in any event a co-defendant cannot use gateway (f).

4.6.1 When Is An Impression False?

The legislation does not set out how to determine whether a false impression has actually been given.[144] In many cases, the judge will need to consider if there is sufficient evidence that shows a false impression has been given (such evidence does not necessarily then go before the jury). In some cases, the decision whether the defendant has given a false impression is in fact one for the jury. In *Renda*, the Court approved this direction: "*If they were sure that he had tried to give a false impression about himself, then the jury was entitled to see how it affected the way in which they should approach the evidence about [the present incident]*".[145]

In *Gabbana*, the Court said that on the facts of the case the jury first needed to be sure that the defendant had given the alleged false impression. However, a failure to do so did not necessarily mean the conviction was unsafe.[146]

A distinction is drawn between bad character evidence being admitted to correct a false impression, which is subject to s.105(1)(b) and s.109,[147] and the basis upon which the judge finds that the defendant has given a

---

144 The Explanatory Notes to the CJA, [376] only contemplate the situation where there is no doubt that what the defendant has said is not actually the case: "*This might be done expressly, for example, by claiming to be of good character when this is not the case, or implied, for example, by leading evidence of his conduct that carries an implication that he is of a better character than is actually the case.*"

145 *Renda* [2005] EWCA Crim 2826, [25]. See also *Maclean* [2024] EWCA Crim 1523, [10]: "*it was for the jury to decide whether Mr Maclean had given a false impression and to do so to the criminal standard*".

146 *Gabbana* [2020] EWCA Crim 1473, [108]-[109].

147 Section 105(1)(b) requires that bad character evidence must have probative value in correcting the false impression, and s.109 requires the court to assume that the evidence is true for the purpose of determining admissibility.

false impression, thus opening the gateway for the admission of the bad character evidence.

Sometimes the two are the same, as, for example, where the defendant asserts that he has never been in trouble with the police, but there are records indicating that he has been cautioned for an offence. In this example, neither the existence of a false impression nor the evidence being used to correct it is in dispute.

The problem arises when the prosecution suggests there has been a false impression based on some evidence that is itself disputed.

There is no false impression when merely contradicting prosecution case. A classic case is where the prosecution says that the defendant is giving a false impression because prosecution evidence already deployed in the case suggests that he is. Plainly, this would be unfair:

> *"The only basis on which it could be said that he was a drug dealer, (in the face of denials of that fact …) was by the very evidence that the Crown wished to adduce, viz. the texts. There was no other evidence to suggest it and it was not a positive case being put by the Crown. The appellant had admitted he was a Class A drug user and he had admitted his past convictions. We therefore cannot see the basis on which the section 101(1)(f) 'gateway' could have been properly invoked."*[148]

Is an impression "*false*" because it is inconsistent with other allegations?

Care should be taken not to distract the jury with satellite litigation by asking them to decide whether other, similar, allegations are true, in order to then use them to correct an alleged false impression.[149]

---

148 *Chrysostomou* [2010] EWCA Crim 1403, [37].

149 This also risks trying to establish propensity by coincidence evidence: see Chapter 6 on cross-admissibility.

This situation arose in *Weir*, where a priest was charged with rape of a female member of his temple. He gave the impression in interview, and via character witnesses, that he had never behaved inappropriately towards female worshippers. The bad character evidence came from two other women (possibly from a different temple) who alleged the defendant made sexually-charged approaches to them. The Court of Appeal said:

> *"In our judgment the evidence of the two women was admissible under section 101(1)(f) because part of the false impression given by the appellant in interview and, as it turned out later by calling seven character witnesses, was that he was a priest who had never behaved inappropriately towards female worshippers at his temple."*[150]

However, the defendant had also denied any inappropriate behaviour towards these two women. This would seem to result in a circularity of use that is liable to confuse rather than assist. The impression is only false if the other, disputed, allegations are true. As stated in *S*,

> "*the result of admitting the evidence in question resulted in a very substantial proportion of the trial being taken up in what might be called a 'collateral' issue relating to the previous behaviour of the appellant; and that type of situation is clearly one which should be avoided if possible so that the issues in the trial do not become distorted.*"[151]

Giving an impression of general good character, or that one is not the sort of person who would commit the present crime might constitute a false impression.

In *Egan*, the defendant (charged with murder and firearms/weapons offences) asserted his good character via evidence that he had entered a burning building in an attempt to rescue elderly and infirm neighbours.

---

150 *Weir* [2005] EWCA Crim 2866, [2006] 1 Cr App R 19, [43].

151 *S* [2007] EWCA Crim 1387, [17].

In response, the Crown successfully relied upon a photograph from the same year, showing the defendant holding a gun to the head of a friend whilst wearing a mask, along with other images of guns.[152]

In *Jalil* the defendant was convicted of conspiracy to murder, in a terrorism-related conspiracy. In chief he stated that he was a businessman working in the mobile telephone industry, and had told this to the police. In cross-examination on his behalf it was asserted that the police had found a business plan for his company while searching his home. The implication was that he was an honest businessman and that the police investigation supported this. Evidence was then admitted under gateway (f) suggesting that the defendant's company was actually being used for fraudulent purposes, possibly carousel or missing trader fraud, unrelated to the alleged terrorist activity.

> *"The judge was entitled to say that the jury would be left with a misleading impression, as a result of the defendant's evidence, if it carried away the message that he was a bona fide businessman and for that reason less likely to be guilty of association with terrorist endeavour."*[153]

See also *Amponsah,* where the defendant was charged with fraudulent evasion of the prohibition on the importation of cocaine, and had a conviction for theft in 1996, but gave an impression of being *"a hard-working, truthful, church-going individual"*. That impression was "*properly balanced by the consideration [that] she had in fact been convicted of an offence of dishonesty."*[154]

---

152 *Egan* [2022] EWCA Crim 392

153 *Jalil* [2008] EWCA Crim 2910, [49]. Arguably, gateway (f) might have worked in this way in *Haigh* [2010] EWCA Crim 90.

154 *Amponsah* [2005] EWCA Crim 2993.

Asserting remorse for the effect (e.g. injury to a victim) of the alleged offending can be a false impression.[155]

Putting partial information before a jury does not necessarily mean one is giving a false impression; it depends on the purpose for which the information is being given. In *Joyce*, D was tried for murder; he argued self-defence. The prosecution had agreed not to put into evidence his character unless gateways (f) or (g) were triggered. At the start of the trial, in cross-examination of a police officer, defence counsel read out a portion of a police log which recorded an anonymous threat made towards D. The log included the line, "*[the caller] described [D] as the king of the travellers and that he is a bare knuckle fighter*". Defence counsel did not read out this sentence as he considered it was evidence of bad character.[156]

After an "*inexplicable*" delay, the prosecution gave notice of intent to rely upon D's convictions, videos of him engaging in bare knuckle fighting, and the full content of the police log including the omitted sentence. The trial judge refused to admit this material. Amongst other reasons, the use of the police log for one purpose (namely to elicit the communication of a potential death threat and what steps the police had taken) did not mean that all of its content must go into evidence. The Court of Appeal agreed.[157]

Does putting forward a defence constitute giving a false impression?

It is clear that a defendant does <u>not</u> give a false impression merely by asserting that he has not committed the present offence. In *Iqbal*, the alleged false impression was the defendant's explanation for why his

---

155 *Phair* [2022] NICA 66, [36].

156 The Court of Appeal agreed that it was: bare knuckle fighting imported bad character and so did the phrase "*king of the travellers*" which "*has connotations and links with bare knuckle fighting*".

157 *Joyce* [2023] NICA 67, [117].

DNA was on a heroin package. The Court of Appeal held that this was not a false impression:

> *"Even if what is contained in a defence case statement can amount to an assertion made by a defendant in the proceedings, the document in reality is setting out the contentions of the defence in relation to a fundamental issue in the case, the nature of his defence and the matters of fact upon which he takes issue. This, in the court's judgment, is not an impression about him, let alone a false or misleading one without begging the very question which the jury would have to determine."*[158]

However, there are some cases where it is not so clear that the defendant is merely presenting his defence. In *H*, D was convicted of five counts of rape of a child and three counts of attempted rape of a child (specimen counts) aged between 7-8.[159] He had numerous previous convictions, including one of a sexual nature against a 17-year old bearing strong similarities to an allegation of oral rape at knifepoint made by C. The judge admitted all convictions via gateways (d) and (f). The latter gateway applied because, in police interviews, D was asked about the allegation that he had held a knife to C's throat at the time he was orally raping her. He said, "*I would not do that*". A little later he said, "*I don't punish her by sticking my dick in her face. That is not the type of person I am*". The prosecution said these statements gave a false impression because it was demonstrable that D had done exactly these things in the past, albeit to someone else.

What is not made clear is whether the knifepoint rape was one of the specimen counts, or part of the general background of events being related by C. If it was one of the specimen counts, then it is arguable that D was merely presenting his defence, i.e. that he did not rape C and, perhaps, would not do such things to her in particular. If so, it would not

158 *Iqbal* [2006] EWCA Crim 1302, [16].

159 *H* [2006] EWCA Crim 2898.

constitute a false impression. On the other hand, if it was not a specimen count, then C's account of the knifepoint rape should not have been allowed in evidence without a separate bad character evidence application. We then face the problem that if D denies an event said to be a part of bad character evidence, can that denial be considered the giving of a false impression and thus the gateway for more bad character evidence? This presents a potentially interminable spiral of bad character evidence.

Asserting that a defendant has no knowledge of gang members or firearms can be a false impression capable of correction. In *Rowe*, the defendant G in cross-examination denied knowing members of two rival gangs and denied knowledge of firearms. The Court of Appeal said that evidence contradicting this was actually s.98(a) evidence, but in any event it was plainly admissible via gateway (f).[160]

In the same case, the defendant J gave evidence that on the day of the incident he had been speaking to his cousin who "*was happy that I'd just finished uni*" in July 2019. The trial judge then observed, presumably in the absence of the jury,

> *"Can I just say before you go on that I was surprised when I heard that comment and I then looked at the antecedents ... There was an impression that he was of a very different character".*

J had pleaded guilty in October 2018 to two offences of the supply of class A drugs in 2016, and was sentenced in November 2019. The Court of Appeal agreed that J had given a false and misleading impression as to his good character and therefore evidence of this conviction was admissible under gateway (f).[161]

It is not immediately clear what the false impression was here. It does not seem to be suggested that J had not in fact been at university. Nor would it be arguable that a person who supplies drugs cannot also complete a

---

160 *Rowe* [2022] EWCA Crim 27, [90]-[91].

161 *Rowe* [2022] EWCA Crim 27, [114]-[117].

year of university. If the real purpose was to give the jury a full understanding of the defendant's character, it may be questioned whether gateway (f) is the proper route for this.

4.6.2 Making, And Withdrawing From, A False Impression

4.6.2.1 Making a false impression

The false impression must be given by the defendant, or be given at his instigation. While this would seem to cover statements made by the defendant, the Court of Appeal has suggested, *obiter*, that there might be an exception where the defendant gives an answer to a direct question in police interview.[162]

Defence counsel can give a false impression that triggers gateway (f). In *Wiseman*, the defendant was charged with fraud by selling, via his church, an oil mixture which he claimed could cure or protect against coronavirus. Defence counsel in his closing speech asserted that the authorities had never previously shown any interest in other items sold by the church. That was not correct: there had been an investigation some four years earlier which did not result in prosecution because the products were withdrawn from sale. The judge properly addressed the issue by correcting what he described as an inadvertent error by counsel (not the defendant) and giving a brief summary of the previous investigation.[163] The jury were carefully warned that this information had no evidential purpose save to cure that error.

Gateway (f) is not likely to be applicable to a statement that is equivocal, or made by "*a defendant in the heat of the moment denying guilt in ill-*

---

[162] *RB* [2008] EWCA Crim 1850, [35]. See also *Good* [2008] EWCA Crim 2923. Perhaps the false impression is not "*given by the defendant*" if it is in response to a leading question by police and is not something the defendant intended to be part of his case at trial.

[163] *Wiseman* [2023] EWCA Crim 1363, [14].

chosen terms which were not intended to secure an undeserved advantage for himself."[164]

In *Cleere*, the Court held that a misleading impression had been given when D1 emphasised "*the positive aspects of [his] character in caring for [a family member] in a devoted manner.*" However, the "*way in which the evidence came out, which was effectively on the spur of the moment in response to cross-examination by a co-defendant's counsel*", meant that the bad character evidence should not have been admitted.[165]

A defendant is less likely to be able to mount such an argument where he has previously been warned by the judge that his character may be admissible if he were to give a false impression.[166]

By s.105(4) and (5), much of the old law dealing with when a defendant makes a statement, including by his clothing or conduct, has been adopted post-CJA. Thus:

- The wearing of a particular clothing, e.g. religious garb or regimental blazer.[167]
- Having an "*extravagant lifestyle*"[168] or possessing large sums of money[169] might be the subject of a false impression if the defendant gives an explanation for them that can be rebutted by bad character evidence, usually in the form of allegations that the defendant engages in criminal activities that produce money.

---

164 *Dunstuan* [2023] EWCA Crim 1632, [25].

165 *Cleere* [2020] EWCA Crim 1360, [18]-[19].

166 *Dunstuan* [2023] EWCA Crim 1632, [24].

167 *Saleem* [2007] EWCA Crim 1923, [22].

168 *Green* [2009] EWCA Crim 1688.

169 *Graham* [2007] EWCA Crim 1499.

However, such cases do tend to risk excessive satellite litigation as well as overlap with disputed evidence that is already part of the prosecution's case against the defendant. The case law has not tended formally to identify these issues as gateway (f) issues.

The gateway is not activated if a defendant gives a false impression about someone or something other than the defendant: s.105(1)(a).

The impression must be *about* the defendant himself, not merely *made by* the defendant. In *Hanson* the judge rejected gateway (f), because the defendant's assertion (that the complainant had a motive to have the defendant removed from the matrimonial home) was not *about the defendant.*[170]

There is a distinction between the defendant making a merely inconsistent statement, or even telling a lie, and the giving of a false impression about himself.

In *Lovelock* there was no false impression about the defendant: he was merely (perhaps unwisely) giving two different reasons for secreting money in another country. He made one statement at trial, and another in an earlier statement. The previous statement he had made about the money could have been adduced to show that he had given a different explanation, and thus to cast doubt on the credibility of his defence. There was no need to treat the second statement in court as a false impression in order to do this.[171]

---

170 *Hanson* [2005] EWCA Crim 824, [2005] 2 Cr App R 21, [51]. See also *Jarvis* [2008] EWCA Crim 488.

171 *Lovelock* [2007] EWCA Crim 476. See also *Stokes* [2015] EWCA Crim 1911, [21] where the Court disagreed that any false impression had been given at all; *Ovba* [2015] EWCA Crim 725, [8], where the impression D gave in evidence that she was a "*friendly person*" was "*far too unspecific and insubstantial*" to trigger gateway (f). Cases where the existence of a false

4.6.2.2 Withdrawing from a false impression

Just as the defendant must be responsible for the making of the false impression, he can also decide to withdraw from it.

Section 105(3) explicitly provides that the defendant will not be treated as being responsible for making an assertion if he "*withdraws or disassociates himself from it.*"

In *Good*, the defendant was not given an opportunity to clarify whether he was asserting something or not, which led to his conviction being quashed.[172]

The defendant in *D, P and U* was convicted of the sexual abuse of his two stepsons. He had stated in interview that he "*preferred females*", but then asked the judge to edit that statement out of the interview so that it would not be adduced. He wished to withdraw any false impression about his sexual preferences that he had given in the interview. The judge refused, saying "*[e]ven if it were edited out, it does not alter the fact that that is what the defendant said and that was his reaction when these allegations were put to him.*" The Court of Appeal corrected this: "*That proposition fell into error because it ignores section 105(3). It also ignores the central proposition to be found in section 105(1)(a) that gateway (f) arises when a false impression is given to the court*",[173] which is to say that it can be prevented from being *given* to the court.

---

impression is doubtful: *Bernasconi* [2006] EWCA Crim 1052; *Jarvis* [2008] EWCA Crim 488; *Eyidah* [2010] EWCA Crim 987.

172 *Good* [2008] EWCA Crim 2923.

173 *D, P and U* [2011] EWCA Crim 1474, [2012] 1 Cr App R 8, [39]. See also *Livesey* [2007] EWCA Crim 361, involving the withdrawal of a planned character statement once the defendant was informed that this would trigger gateway (f).

The proper application of s.105(3) was confirmed in *Khan*, where the defendant's denial in interview that he supplied drugs was given in the context of being accused of selling drugs in a hostel. This was still capable of being a false impression, because "*to the extent that it was an implied assertion that he was not the sort of person who would ever supply another with Class A drugs, it was untrue.*" But the Court said, quashing the conviction,[174]

> *"In these circumstances, we can see no good reason why the record of the interview could not have been further edited, under section 105(6), so as to remove references to any more general implied assertion that he was not the sort of person who supplied drugs, so as to correct any false impression. … Nor do we understand why the judge thought that the evidence would be bound to come out. It was certainly not in the interests of the appellant to raise it, and we cannot see how the prosecution could have put questions with the intention of eliciting a damaging admission which would introduce the appellant's previous conviction."*[175]

The principle in s.105(3) would seem straightforward, except for a few cases such as *H*,[176] where the judge refused to allow the defendant to edit an interview record to remove the false impression he was alleged to have made, so as to avoid his convictions being put in evidence. In *Dixon* the Court of Appeal stated:

> *"We reject [the defendant's] assertion that the proper way to correct any false impression created by the appellant in interview was to edit the interview. This is to miss the point. The evidence of what he had said when confronted by the allegations was relevant and admissible. If an accused lies in interview and the consequences for the appellant*

[174] On this basis and on the basis of a separate misdirection to the jury.

[175] *Khan* [2020] EWCA Crim 163, [20].

[176] *H* [2006] EWCA Crim 2898.

> *are unfortunate, the answer is not to edit out those lies. The answer is that the prosecution is entitled to rely upon those lies."*[177]

The purpose and effect of s.105(3) does not support this interpretation. It might be that these cases are outliers, given the rest of the case law. In so far as gateway (f) and false impressions are concerned, the "*proper way*" is indeed to edit the interview or otherwise to allow the defendant to withdraw or disassociate from the "*lie*" in the interview. The Explanatory Notes make it clear that the defendant was not intended to be allowed to use s.101(3) to request the exclusion of gateway (f) evidence, because he can achieve the same effect by withdrawing or disassociating himself from the false impression.[178] Exclusion, then, is the function of s.105(3). Of course, this does not prevent another gateway from operating to allow those convictions into evidence, provided that gateway's conditions are satisfied, as in fact happened in *Dixon* (via gateway (g)).

4.6.3 How Much Evidence Is Required To Correct A False Impression?

It has already been observed that gateway (f) lends itself to a circularity of use. The possibility was mentioned in *D, P and U*,[179] and can be observed in *Gillespie*.[180] There, the defendant was held to have given a false impression in respect of other bad character evidence which was already going to be admitted via gateway (d). This suggests a potential cyclical use of s.101. In that sense, there is no limit on gateway (f) (as there is on

---

177 *Dixon* [2012] EWCA Crim 2163, [17].

178 Explanatory Notes to the CJA, [378]: "*A defendant may withdraw or disassociate himself from a false or misleading impression. Evidence to correct the impression is not then admissible: section 105(3). In light of this, section 101(3), under which a defendant may apply to have evidence of his bad character excluded, does not apply to this evidence.*"

179 *D, P and U* [2011] EWCA Crim 1474, [2012] 1 Cr App R 8, [39].

180 *Gillespie* [2011] EWCA Crim 3152.

gateways (c), (d) and (e)), that the false impression or the bad character evidence has to be relevant to the trial.

There is one limit, however, that is important and unusual. It is that the scope and application of any evidence admitted via gateway (f) is very specific—it can only be evidence that has probative value in correcting the false impression, and may not go any further than is necessary to correct that false impression.[181] Bad character, therefore, is divisible for the purposes of gateway (f).[182] In order to comply with s.105(6), references to bad character should be removed where appropriate.[183]

In *Reid*, reference to unproved allegations were plainly prejudicial and "*could not possibly assist the jury*" to decide whether he had given a false impression of his changed character.[184] Section 105(6) requires a "*rigorous approach*". In the same case, references to his former solicitors' notes[185] had little relevance in correcting any impression the defendant might be said to have given of the things said by or to the solicitors.[186]

The application of s.105(6) is fairly wide.

In *Uyiekpen*, the defendant's conviction for possessing class A drugs with intent to supply was quashed because the defendant had not been permitted to give evidence that he had no convictions for drug-related offences. The fact that he had a conviction for assault, and was facing trial

---

[181] Section 105(1)(b) and (6).

[182] *Weir* [2005] EWCA Crim 2866, [2006] 1 Cr App R 19, [43]: "*We accept that [s 105(6)] is a statutory reversal of the previous common law position that character is indivisible*".

[183] *Lovelock* [2007] EWCA Crim 476.

[184] *Reid* [2024] EWCA Crim 308, [43].

[185] Privilege having apparently been waived, although the CACD expressed doubt about this.

[186] *Reid* [2024] EWCA Crim 308, [45].

on charges of robbery and false imprisonment, did not detract from the accuracy of the assertion that he had no drug-related convictions. It was not a false impression to state that he had no previous convictions relating to drugs, and evidence of some pending charges "*was simply not admissible.*"[187]

In *Spartley*, D said in interview that he had "*not been in trouble with police before and would not involve himself in an enterprise of the kind suggested*" (importation of drugs).[188] Evidence was admitted via gateway (f) to the effect that, seven years previously, he had been <u>interviewed</u> by Dutch police in relation to a cannabis investigation (no charges or convictions resulted). Was this a gateway (f) case? Arguably, D's false impression was stating that he would not involve himself in an enterprise involving drug importation or supply. The Dutch evidence was not proof that he had done so. Was the false impression instead saying that he had not been in trouble with police? Is being interviewed by the police equivalent to being in trouble with them?

Wylie suggests that these subtle distinctions may well be permissible, and even necessary, under gateway (f).[189] D had never been arrested or interviewed by the police before, but he did have a conviction for a company-related offence that had been investigated by the Official Receiver. Thus, it was agreed with the prosecution that D could say, when asked, that he had never been in trouble *with the police* before.[190] This would not trigger gateway (f).

---

187 *Uyiekpen* [2008] EWCA Crim 1457, [13].

188 *Spartley* [2007] EWCA Crim 1789, [14]. These are the Court's words—the exact phrase used in interview was not quoted.

189 *Wylie* [2010] EWCA Crim 3110.

190 Unfortunately, when he was actually questioned about the periphery of the previous matter, the defendant answered that he had "*never been in trouble before*", rather than that he had "*never been in trouble with the police*

If such a distinction can be made in *Wylie*, then presumably the opposite distinction can also be made (in a case such as *Spartley*) between different police forces and, even, the subject of that "*trouble*", whether it is mere questioning, arrest or a formal charge.

A partial qualification to the divisibility of character is the scenario in *H*, where, on trial for murder, D gave evidence in-chief of his practice of buying and selling stolen cars. In light of his lengthy record of more serious offences, including offences of serious violence and possession of bladed articles, the impression D had given about his bad character was misleading. A number (not all) of those serious convictions were therefore admissible under gateway (f).[191]

Finally, in *Omotoso*, the defendant's mis-statement in examination-in-chief as to the nature of his work did not convey a false impression that needed to be corrected by any bad character evidence. "*If there was real and justifiable concern about what [D] had said and the impression it might have conveyed, it could and should have been corrected in some form of admission as to what he had been doing*", which was unrelated to his bad character.[192] Further, the prosecution should have made any gateway (f) argument while the defendant was still giving evidence, and not after the defence had closed its case.

4.7 Gateway (g): S.101(1)(g)

"(g) the defendant has made an attack on another person's character"

"106 'Attack on another person's character'

---

before"! The prosecution was then permitted to adduce details of the previous conviction.

191 *H* [2018] EWCA Crim 2868, [2019] 1 Cr App R 25.

192 *Omotoso* [2018] EWCA Crim 1394, [51].

(1) For the purposes of section 101(1)(g) a defendant makes an attack on another person's character if—

> *(a) he adduces evidence attacking the other person's character,*
>
> *(b) he (or any legal representative appointed under section 38(4) of the Youth Justice and Criminal Evidence Act 1999 (c. 23) to cross-examine a witness in his interests) asks questions in cross-examination that are intended to elicit such evidence, or are likely to do so, or*
>
> *(c) evidence is given of an imputation about the other person made by the defendant—*
>
> > *(i) on being questioned under caution, before charge, about the offence with which he is charged, or*
> >
> > *(ii) on being charged with the offence or officially informed that he might be prosecuted for it.*

(2) In subsection (1) 'evidence attacking the other person's character' means evidence to the effect that the other person—

> *(a) has committed an offence (whether a different offence from the one with which the defendant is charged or the same one), or*
>
> *(b) has behaved, or is disposed to behave, in a reprehensible way; and 'imputation about the other person' means an assertion to that effect.*

(3) Only prosecution evidence is admissible under section 101(1)(g)."

4.7.1 *Credibility*

Gateway (g) contains no express reason for the admission of the bad character evidence. That the other substantive gateways do is clear from their wording: gateways (c), (d), (e) and (f) begin with reference to evidence of the defendant's bad character (they all begin with "*it*"), followed by some reason why that evidence is admissible. But gateway (g) makes no reference to the evidence. Nor does s.106.

Its predecessor, the second part of s.1(1)(f)(ii) of the Criminal Evidence Act 1898, reads, in context:

> *"A person charged in criminal proceedings who is called as a witness in the proceedings shall not be asked, and if asked shall not be required to answer, any question tending to show that he has committed or been convicted of or been charged with any offence other than one with which he is then charged, or is of bad character, unless … the nature or conduct of the defence is such as to involve imputations on the character of the prosecutor or the witnesses for the prosecution."*

The case law on this provision indicated that the purpose of tit-for-tat character attacks was to level the playing field between the credibility of two witnesses: a defendant who gives evidence and the prosecution witness whose character he attacks.[193]

The idea of evening-out the playing field is still the central purpose of gateway (g).[194] Although there is nothing in the words of gateway (g) or s.106 to suggest it, the gateway has become, by default, about the defendant's own credibility. Thus: if the jury does not have character information for *both* sides in a credibility assessment task, the verdict may be unsafe.

---

193 This guide has not dwelt on pre-CJA law for obvious reasons. Most old cases are now no longer helpful: in *Littlechild* [2006] EWCA Crim 2126 the Court said it was "*very dangerous*" to interpret gateway (g) using the pre-CJA case of *Selvey v DPP* [1970] AC 304. See also *Platt* [2016] EWCA Crim 4, [23]-[29].

194 E.g. *McPherson* [2010] EWCA Crim 2906, [12].

Not everything a defendant says or asserts means that the playing field has been tilted in his favour.[195] The tit-for-tat approach should be used only where it is "*truly required*".[196]

In *Williams*, although the judge did not "*focus as clearly as he might on the distinction between 101(1)(d) and 101(1)(g)*", his decision to admit offences of dishonesty was correct.

> *"In a case where the defence had launched an attack on the character of the prosecution witnesses the jury were entitled to know about the character of the defendant and in particular that he had offences of dishonesty in deciding whether or not to believe his evidence rather than that of the prosecution witnesses."*[197]

In *Brewster*, the Court allowed an appeal against convictions for kidnapping and theft, on the basis that the judge should have admitted evidence of the complainant's bad character, including a conviction for manslaughter. If this had been done, the defendants' bad character would also have been put into evidence, each having "*criminal records of some seriousness*".[198] It was very possible that "*if the jury had learned of the*

---

195 It might be argued that a defendant is the first victim of the tit-for-tat game: he comes to trial only because the prosecutor has chosen to make an attack on his character (i.e. accusing him of a crime). The presumption of innocence is there to remind the tribunal of fact to avoid placing the accused in a disadvantaged position because of the fact that he has been accused.

196 Lord Hope in *DS v Her Majesty's Advocate* [2007] UKPC D1, [43] said, when looking for comparative guidance from the legislation of England and Wales, that "*the court is required by that scheme to have regard to certain specific factors designed to* limit *the introduction of evidence on a tit-for-tat basis to those cases where it is truly required*" (emphasis added).

197 *Williams* [2007] EWCA Crim 1951, [28]; and see *O'Sullivan* [2013] EWCA Crim 43, [19]. But see *Hearne* [2009] EWCA Crim 103.

198 *Brewster* [2010] EWCA Crim 1194, [2010] 2 Cr App R 20, [25].

convictions of each of the main actors at trial" they would have reached a different verdict. "*[T]he jury might have been persuaded that they could not safely act on [the complainant's] evidence notwithstanding the bad character of the accused.*"[199]

Note that gateway (g) does not require that anyone gives evidence before it is triggered. However, where the attack is on a non-witness who is also a non-victim, s.101(3) should normally be exercised to exclude the evidence.[200]

Even if gateway (g) is triggered, it does not follow that all aspects of the defendant's bad character must be admitted. The judge can and should consider exclusion of each item of bad character under the exclusionary provisions (see Chapter 5). For example, in *Guthrie*, the defendant's allegation that C had invented the whole incident meant that his "*entire character was capable of being adduced under (g)*", but "*[i]n order to avoid undue prejudice however the learned judge fairly ruled that offences relating to driving and dishonesty would not be admitted.*"[201]

4.7.2 Using Evidence After Admission

Balancing credibility is not the sole purpose of gateway (g).

Highton was asked to address the question:

> "*whether evidence admitted under s.101(1)(g) … is admissible as evidence of a propensity to commit offences of the kind with which the defendant is charged, or is only admissible in relation to his*

199 *Brewster* [2010] EWCA Crim 1194, [2010] 2 Cr App R 20, [25].

200 *Nelson* [2006] EWCA Crim 3412, [16].

201 *Guthrie* [2016] EWCA Crim 1633, [14].

> *credibility, that is, as evidence tending to show that he is likely to be untruthful."*[202]

In response, the Court held that bad character evidence admitted via gateway (g) can be used for whatever relevant purpose exists.

> *"In the case of gateway (g), for example, admissibility depends on the defendant having made an attack on another person's character, but once the evidence is admitted, it may, depending on the particular facts, be relevant not only to credibility but also to propensity to commit offences of the kind with which the defendant is charged."*[203]

Highton therefore tells us that gateway (g) evidence *can* be relevant to propensity. It will not always be relevant.[204]

Thus, for example:

- Gateway (a) evidence can be used for both s.103(1)(a) and (b) types of propensity.[205] As to *Highton* and gateways (a) and (b) more generally, see above.

---

202 *Highton* [2005] EWCA Crim 1985, [2006] 1 Cr App R 7, [1].

203 *Highton* [2005] EWCA Crim 1985, [2006] 1 Cr App R 7, [10]. This last is a reference to the gateway (d) matter in issue of propensity (s.103(1)(a)).

204 *Williams* [2011] EWCA Crim 2198, [14]. The convictions in question were "*relevant to the purpose for which they were sought to be admitted under gateway (g)*" (i.e. whether D was more worthy of belief than the police officers whose character he had attacked), but were not, and could not have been, relied upon as evidence of propensity. However, "*there was a clear and considerable risk of the jury treating them as such once the jury knew about them.*"

205 *Gourde* [2009] EWCA Crim 1803. This case shows it is advisable to agree the exact uses of the evidence before agreeing to use gateway (a).

- Gateway (d) evidence can be used as gateway (c) evidence, where (c) was not otherwise satisfied: *Doncaster.*[206]

- Gateway (d) evidence can be used towards credibility in the gateway (g) sense, where a separate gateway (g) argument was rejected.[207]

- Evidence admitted as relevant to one important matter in issue (under gateway (d)) can then be used for another gateway (d) purpose even if it would not have been admissible for that second purpose. In *Campbell* the important matter in issue was a propensity to commit domestic violence offences. The bad character evidence could then be used for a credibility purpose, not because s.103(1)(b) was satisfied (it was not) but because "*[o]nce the evidence has been admitted through a gateway it is open to the jury to attach significance to it in any respect in which it is relevant.*"[208] This is subject to the important requirement that the court must decide what those relevant uses are and must direct the jury on them.[209]

The *Highton* principle is not clear-cut. *Highton* arose because the Court was asked whether evidence admitted under gateway (g) can be used, for example, for a gateway (d) purpose. Because the other gateways generally have readily-identifiable parameters (unlike gateway (g)), it is not always

---

206 *Doncaster* [2008] EWCA Crim 5.

Hassett [2008] EWCA Crim 1634, [29]: A credibility use is equivalent to a gateway (g) use. The judge directed "*that the convictions ... go not only to propensity but also to credibility*", which the Court of Appeal said meant "*that which had been admitted by reference to gateway (d) [as going to propensity] was also relevant now to gateway (g) [thus going also to credibility]. There is authority permitting such an approach: see* R v Highton".

208 *Campbell* [2007] EWCA Crim 1472, [2007] 2 Cr App R 28, [25].

209 *D, P and U* [2011] EWCA Crim 1474, [2012] 1 Cr App R 8, [3].

appropriate to ask whether evidence admitted via those gateways can be used for a different purpose.

As a result, many cases limit or contradict the above uses.[210] For example:

- The judge retains the power to confine the uses of the evidence.[211]

- Evidence admitted under gateway (c) should not readily be used for a purpose such as propensity for which additional safeguards and different tests have first to be met.[212]

- A judge who is minded to direct the jury that a conviction is relevant to propensity must apply the principles in *Hanson*.[213] This would seem to narrow *Highton* considerably.

---

210 There are many texts discussing whether *Highton* was correctly decided. This text confines such discussion to practical points that may assist.

211 *Lamaletie and Royce* [2008] EWCA Crim 314, [13].

212 *Davis* [2008] EWCA Crim 1156, [2009] 2 Cr App R 17, [34]. *Davis* is suggesting that the *Highton* approach is only permissible if the admitting gateway is more stringent than the gateway(s) that would lead to different usages. Thus a party cannot use an easier gateway to allow a usage that belongs to a more difficult gateway. It seeks to confine *Highton* to situations where admissibility is achieved via gateways (d) and (g) only. In the situation of gateway (c), while "*it would seem difficult to think that the jury should be limited in its use*", there is also a "*danger*" in admitting evidence via gateway (c) if the intended use is really as evidence of propensity, "*where the statutory tests and safeguards are different*" at [36]. The Court then cites a number of cases for the proposition that gateway (c) should not be subject to the *Highton* principle.

213 *Fryer and Tedstone* [2006] EWCA Crim 1530.

- Gateways (d) and (e) have separate identities, specify a standard of relevance to something[214] and by default should be used for that purpose.[215]

- Gateway (f) evidence is particularly unlikely to be capable of any other uses. In *Parsons* the defendant's previous convictions had been admitted under gateway (f) to rebut his false assertion in chief that he had never been to court before. There was a potential other usage because one conviction was for possession of cannabis, and the present charge was for supplying cannabis. The judge should have directed the jury that the convictions could not be used for a s.103(1)(a) propensity purpose, and that the convictions were only before the jury in order to "*cure the false impression*".[216] There was no mention of *Highton* at all. It might be inferred that the Court considered that s.105(6) negated any applicability of *Highton*. Gateway (f) has an explicit *limitation* on the scope of the evidence and its usage. Section 105(6) in fact links the question of 'admissibility' with that of 'usage': if the evidence could go (meaning could 'achieve', or 'be used for') further

214 E.g. an important matter in issue.

215 *Lawson* [2006] EWCA Crim 2572, [2007] 1 Cr App R 11, [35] described the differences between gateways (d) and (e): "*It is quite apparent from the shape of this Act that although it uses the expression 'propensity for untruthfulness' in both section 103(1)(b) in relation to prosecution applications and in section 104(1) in relation to applications by co-accused, it addresses the various different occasions on which bad character may arguably be admissible separately and provides a* different framework of rules for each situation" (emphasis added). See also *Singh* [2007] EWCA Crim 2140, [9]: "*The Act plainly demonstrates that the gateways are independent, although of course in some cases more than one of them may be passed.*"

216 *Parsons* [2011] EWCA Crim 2591. See also *Yousefi* [2020] EWCA Crim 791; *Cudjoe* [2012] EWCA Crim 3062, [15]-[17]; *Weir* [2005] EWCA Crim 2866, [2006] 1 Cr App R 19, [43].

than is necessary to correct the false impression, then it is not even admissible.

- The prosecution should not ordinarily seek to use *Highton* to rely on evidence that has been admitted by a defendant via gateway (e) or (c). When D2 adduces evidence of D1's bad character, "*it is to be hoped that the prosecution do not seek in closing the case to the jury to rely on it*",[217] unless the evidence is also admissible via a prosecution gateway. This principle was not followed in *Stokes* where, apparently by agreement, evidence admitted under gateway (e) could be used by all parties "*as they sought fit*", despite a prosecution application to admit the same bad character evidence having earlier been refused.[218]

- *Highton* "*does not relieve the court of the duty of establishing which gateway or gateways are applicable*",[219] because (1) this ensures that bad character evidence "*is only admitted when the statute allows it*", and (2) "*the decision as to the relevant gateway or gateways will normally be of great help in identifying the way or ways in which the evidence can legitimately be used—that is to say the issues to which it is relevant.*" This ensures that the evidence is used only "*on any issue to which it is legitimately relevant*", and not merely "*in any way the jury chooses.*" The application of these principles is clear in the case of *D.*[220] The bad character evidence undoubtedly passed gateway (g), but because it had the potential to be used for propensity purposes as well, gateway (d) needed to be considered.

---

217 *Robinson* [2005] EWCA Crim 3233, [2006] 1 Cr App R 32.

218 *Stokes* [2018] EWCA Crim 1350, [29].

219 *D, P and U* [2011] EWCA Crim 1474, [2012] 1 Cr App R 8, [3].

220 *D, P and U* [2011] EWCA Crim 1474, [2012] 1 Cr App R 8, beginning at [24].

> This would allow the judge to determine how the jury should be directed.

Arguably, *Highton* is needed only in those situations where the gateway (g) usage is unclear, or where there is an unavoidable overlap between the gateway (g) usage and the gateway (d) conditions.

Thus, in *Lafayette* the Court distinguished the situation where bad character evidence admitted under gateway (g) is also admissible under gateway (d) (meaning that both sets of *admission* criteria are satisfied), from the situation where evidence admissible under gateway (g) is not admissible under gateway (d) to show propensity.

> *In many cases at least some of the bad character evidence admitted under gateway (g) will also be admissible under gateway (d) and thus entitle the judge to give a propensity direction (see* Highton *...). What is the position to-day if the evidence which is admissible under gateway (g) is not admissible under gateway (d) to show propensity? For example, what should the judge say if the evidence under gateway (g) showed only previous convictions for offences of dishonesty and/or drugs offences and/or offences of violence, from any of which the jury would not be entitled to conclude that they showed on the part of the defendant a propensity to commit the kind of offences with which he is charged?*[221]

The first situation entitles the judge to give a propensity direction, whereas the second does not. *"[T]he better course is for the direction to be so fashioned in a gateway (g) only case that the jury understand that the relevance of these kinds of previous convictions goes to credit and they should not consider that it shows a propensity to commit the offence they are considering, at least if there is a risk that they might do so."*

Chrysostomou expounds a cautious approach to usage after gateway (g) (in particular requiring some probative value beyond blackening the

[221] *Lafayette* [2008] EWCA Crim 3238, [49].

defendant's general character): "*In our view, the texts had no relevance other than to blacken the general character of the appellant in the eyes of the jury and, therefore, dent the credibility of his evidence generally.*"[222]

The problem of gateway (g) might be said to be captured by the direction in *Noble*:

> *"Now, you heard about [D's bad character], members of the jury, because there have been attacks on the characters of prosecution witnesses in this case. And in those circumstances, it is only right that you should hear something of the character of the persons making that attack. But you may feel, members of the jury, that in the context of this case—given firstly that those matters were a long time ago where [D] would have been very young—they do not add anything to this case. And you may think in the circumstances that you can ignore them. Certainly, members of the jury, you must not assume in any way that a defendant is guilty just because he has previous convictions. And you may think that in the circumstances here, as I say, they do not take the matter any further at all."*[223]

In light of that assessment, it might be queried what the purpose of admitting this evidence was.

Given the variety of approaches above, it is good practice to consider whether the use of gateway (g) evidence for additional purposes is compatible with a fair trial and will not distract the jury from the main issues in the case.

There may remain a power to exclude evidence.[224]

---

222 *Chrysostomou* [2010] EWCA Crim 1403, [40].

223 *Noble* [2016] EWCA Crim 2219, [80].

224 See Chapter 5 gateway (g) discussion.

4.7.3 What Is Evidence Attacking Another Person's Character?

This largely mirrors the definition of bad character given by s.98 and s.112(1), except that there is no s.98(a) equivalent.

Section 106(1)(a) refers to "*evidence attacking the other person's character*".

This is defined in s.106(2) as:

1. Evidence "*to the effect that*" the other person has committed an offence.

    a. This offence can be any conviction or allegation.

    b. It can include the offence with which the defendant is charged.

2. Evidence "*to the effect that*" the other person has behaved or is disposed to behave in a reprehensible way. The meaning of "*reprehensible*" should be interpreted in line with the definition of "*misconduct*" in s.112(1).[225]

3. An "*imputation*" about a person means an assertion to that effect. This is intended to capture mere allegations, accusations, and otherwise unsupported statements about a person.[226] No proof from the defendant as to the accusation is required before gateway (g) is triggered.

An important note about the above definition is that it does <u>not</u> exclude evidence that falls within s.98(a). Thus, an attack on someone's character that is to do with the alleged facts of the offence (typically, if the defendant accuses the complainant of lying, or of initiating a fight) can still

---

[225] See Chapter 2.

[226] E.g. that a witness was "*evil, vindictive and violent, she drank too much, had a vendetta against him, told malicious lies about him, and had even taken out a contract on his life*": *JP* [2016] EWCA Crim 1331, [50].

trigger gateway (g). Whether it *should* do so in any individual case will be a matter for argument. Section 101(3) should be used to avoid unfairness towards a defendant who reasonably needs to make such accusations in pursuit of his defence.

In *Thomas*, an attack on C's credibility by reference to her previous false allegation (for a similar crime but against a different defendant) engaged gateway (g). It was not necessary for D to give evidence before his bad character could be put into evidence in response to the attack. Nor was it unfair to place D in a position where he could avoid his bad character being admitted if he did not give evidence. That approach was generous to D, as gateway (g) had already been engaged by the attack on C.[227]

In *Yaryare*, the Court held that cross-examination of a police officer which suggested that the officer's evidence was in part "*false or based on deliberately exaggerated testimony*", and that she was "*intent on getting a conviction and keeping her reputation intact*" was sufficient to trigger gateway (g).[228]

Yaryare was an extreme instance of attacking a police officer. Merely suggesting that the investigation was flawed is unlikely to be sufficient. In *Omotoso*, the Court said that gateway (g) should not be invoked too lightly so as to inhibit a legitimate line of questioning of a police officer:

> *"It may be that cross-examination of a police officer to suggest that his investigation was flawed may amount to an attack on his character, but judges should be careful to ensure that gateway (g) is not invoked too lightly in such cases, and thereby inhibit a legitimate line of questioning. A gentle hint should be sufficient to alert trial counsel of the potential dangers of pursuing a particular course. Although the Judge recognised that undermining a police officer's evidence might be legitimate, he drew a distinction where it went 'beyond the issues*

---

227 *Thomas* [2020] EWCA Crim 4.

228 *Yaryare* [2020] EWCA Crim 1314, [2020] 4 WLR 156, [101]-[102].

> *in the case'. Plainly gratuitous insults should not be permitted in the course of cross-examination and may lead to the revelation of the defendant's character under gateway (g), but the Judge gave no examples of how the questioning suggested that the officer failed to do his job properly or how the cross-examination went beyond the issues in the case."*[229]

As for blaming others for the offence, see *Walker*, where D was on trial for the manslaughter of a baby, and sought in interview to blame a paramedic for the death. The judge "*was not persuaded that it would be right*" to admit D's bad character under gateway (g).[230]

4.7.4 *How Is An Attack Made?*

An attack on another person's character can be made in a number of ways:

- A direct attack by evidence: s.106(1)(a). E.g. giving oral evidence that 'person A has a conviction for assault'. This is the most common way of attacking someone else's character and makes the triggering of gateway (g) obvious.

- Cross-examining a witness (on behalf of the defendant) in such a way as to elicit an attack on someone's character: s.106(1)(b). Thus, asking a police officer, 'Can you confirm that person A has a conviction for assault?' This provision is rarely used without an agreed position being discussed in advance (i.e. D agrees to sacrifice his shield in exchange for this evidence). The words at the end of s.106(1)(b), "*or are likely to do so*", do not add much. They cover the circumstance where the content of the attack is evident

---

229 *Omotoso* [2018] EWCA Crim 1394, [59].

230 *Walker* [2019] EWCA Crim 1825, [23].

from the question but the witness does not actually give the desired answer.

- Evidence is given at trial of an imputation the defendant made about the other person before the trial. Commonly, this covers the situation where the defendant alleges something about person A during his police interview or upon charge. The key here is that the evidence of that imputation needs to be "*given*" at the trial. It is not enough that the defendant *made* the imputation. This is akin to the gateway (f) provision which states that a false impression can be withdrawn and not relied upon.

An attack must be made in the presence of the jury. Statements made on behalf of the defence in the absence of the jury (e.g. in an abuse argument) cannot form the basis of an argument under gateway (g).[231]

In *Nelson* the Court held that the judge was wrong to allow gateway (g) to apply to the defendant's comments in a police interview, because they were not relevant and should not have been admitted. The judge did not properly address why the defendant's objection to the "*giving*" of the evidence should not be upheld.

> *"It is, in our view, difficult to see what relevance to the issues before the jury the appellant's comments in interview about [the victim's friend] could have had. Certainly it would be improper for the prosecution to seek to get such comments before a jury simply to provide a basis for satisfying gateway (g) and getting the defendant's previous convictions put in evidence. We do not seek to suggest that that was the motivation of the prosecution in this case but nonetheless, objectively speaking, that seems to us to have been the situation which*

231 *Omotoso* [2018] EWCA Crim 1394, [53].

> *arose. It follows that, in our judgment, this was not a proper basis for meeting the requirements of gateway (g) on admissibility."*[232]

However, contrast *Hanson* (*Pickstone*) where the defendant made a character attack on C in interview, which the Court described as a "*self-serving assertion*":

> *"Nor do we accept that the evidence had to be excluded because the defendant was not warned at the time of the interview of the possible consequences of what he said. Anyone who makes a self-serving assertion of significance in interview can expect the Crown to seek to adduce, at the subsequent trial, relevant and admissible evidence to refute it. In this case, that included the evidence of the defendant's earlier conviction."*[233]

Of course, such warnings are not required at police stations (unlike s.34 warnings under the Criminal Justice and Public Order Act 1994 (CJPOA)). It might seem harsh that a defendant cannot choose to resile from what may have been an unguarded or heated accusation that he does not now rely on at trial.

Note that there is no requirement that the attack made by the defendant is unjust or unfounded. The statement that triggers gateway (g) might be completely accurate and undisputed. This does not protect the defendant against the admission of his own bad character.

Merely putting a defence (as opposed to making gratuitous attacks that have limited relevance) can still cause a defendant to lose his shield. In *Benabbou*, the Court agreed that the defence case unavoidably involved attacking prosecution witnesses, and that this also ran the inevitable risk

---

232 *Nelson* [2006] EWCA Crim 3412, [19].

233 *Hanson* [2005] EWCA Crim 824, [2005] 2 Cr App R 21, [52]. However, note that an attack on another is not always "*a self-serving assertion*".

of facilitating admission of a prior conviction.[234] An exclusionary provision such as s.101(3) should play a role here to prevent unfairness to the defendant.[235]

However, a distinction should be drawn between the *Benabbou* scenario and a case where the defence merely calls or relies on evidence that undermines or is inconsistent with what a prosecution witness has said.[236] The latter is not an attack that triggers gateway (g).

[234] *Benabbou* [2012] EWCA Crim 1256, [28].

[235] See its importance in *Omotoso* [2018] EWCA Crim 1394, [61]-[62].

[236] *Omotoso* [2018] EWCA Crim 1394, [60], referring to the calling of evidence that "*was intended to undermine the evidence of the officer in the case*".

CHAPTER FIVE

EXCLUSIONS

This Chapter deals with the exclusion of bad character evidence that has passed the initial admissibility test (i.e. a gateway in Chapters 3 and 4). It focuses on the statutory exclusions for prosecution evidence, and then deals with some specific issues arising in respect of defence evidence. It also examines the remedial or exclusionary options provided by s.107 and s.108.

The only formal exclusions are those in s.101(3)/s.101(4) and s.103(3).

However, s.78 of PACE is also applicable to prosecution evidence admitted via s.98(a) or (b), s.100, and s.101.

There are no formal exclusionary provisions in relation to bad character evidence admitted at the behest of a defendant. Gateway (e) has a pseudo-exclusion, dealt with at the end of this Chapter.

5.1 Statutory Provisions

Section 101(3) reads:

> *"The court must not admit evidence under subsection (1)(d) or (g) if, on an application by the defendant to exclude it, it appears to the court that the admission of the evidence would have such an adverse effect on the fairness of the proceedings that the court ought not to admit it."*

Section 101(4) elaborates:

> *"On an application to exclude evidence under subsection (3) the court must have regard, in particular, to the length of time between*

> *the matters to which that evidence relates and the matters which form the subject of the offence charged."*

Section 103(3) reads:

> *"(3) Subsection (2) [referring to a defendant's propensity to commit offences of the kind with which he is charged] does not apply in the case of a particular defendant if the court is satisfied, by reason of the length of time since the conviction or for any other reason, that it would be unjust for it to apply in his case."*

Section 78 reads:

> *"Exclusion of unfair evidence*
>
> *(1) In any proceedings the court may refuse to allow evidence on which the prosecution proposes to rely to be given if it appears to the court that, having regard to all the circumstances, including the circumstances in which the evidence was obtained, the admission of the evidence would have such an adverse effect on the fairness of the proceedings that the court ought not to admit it.*
>
> *(2) Nothing in this section shall prejudice any rule of law requiring a court to exclude evidence."*

By s.112(1), *"prosecution evidence"* means evidence which is to be (or has been) adduced by the prosecution, or which a witness is to be invited to give (or has given) in cross-examination by the prosecution.

5.2 Section 78 Of PACE

Summary:

- If seeking to exclude bad character evidence, it is advisable to rely on s.101(3) instead of s.78 for gateways (d) and (g).[1] Both can be argued, but as they largely duplicate the same concept, failure on one is likely to mean failure on the other.

- Section 78 can be used when the defendant wishes to oppose the prosecution's use of gateways (c) or (f) (as s.101(3) does not assist here).

- Section 78 applies to any prosecution evidence that falls within the s.98 exceptions (s.98(a) and (b)), as such evidence is not evidence of bad character.[2]

- Section 78 applies to prosecution evidence admitted under s.100.

- Gateway (e) cannot be subject to s.78, because it cannot be used to admit prosecution evidence.

5.2.1 The Interplay Between S.101(3) and S.78

Early cases were unclear on this point.[3] However, the position is now clearer and s.78 is regularly used in respect of prosecution evidence of bad character, however admitted.

---

1 Because the power in s.101(3) is explicit and refers only to two gateways, it may have been intended that there should be no other power that could disallow evidence admitted via any other gateway.

2 *McPherson* [2010] EWCA Crim 2906, [16].

3 *Davis* [2008] EWCA Crim 1156, [2009] 2 Cr App R 17, [36].

Section 78 is broader (a generalised provision), designed to deal with any problem the court may face (including illegitimate means of obtaining evidence), whereas s.101(3) and (4) are tailored specifically to the use of bad character evidence, and contemplate the use of evidence that dates from some time in the past.

Section 101(3) requires an application by the defendant, whereas s.78 is a provision that should be in the court's contemplation at all times, even if it decides not to exercise the power therein. Similarly, s.103(3) does not require an application by the defendant.[4]

Section 78 is written in an optional style ("*may refuse*") whereas s.101(3) is mandatory ("*must not*"). *Hanson* suggests that s.101(3) is a stronger provision than s.78 PACE, because the words "*must not admit*" carry a greater imperative than "*may refuse to allow*".[5] On the other hand, the interpretation in *Tirnaveanu* of the pre-CJA case of *Chalkley* suggests that although s.78 ("*may refuse*") seems to import more discretion, both are still essentially mandatory provisions, containing the words "*ought not to admit*".[6] Most discussions tend to treat both provisions as equivalent. In

4 Thus D's request in *Miller* [2010] EWCA Crim 1578 that the judge not consider s.103(3) at all, for tactical reasons, causes some problems. *Miller* concerned the rape of the defendant's 11-year-old niece. While a teenager in 1997, D was convicted of the gang rape of a 15-year-old acquaintance. P wished to use this conviction for s.103(1)(a) purposes. D objected, but asked the judge to confine himself to the s.103(1)(a) propensity question and not to consider s.103(3) or s.78. This was because D wanted to suggest that his niece had made a false complaint against him while knowing that his 1997 conviction would support her.

5 *Hanson* [2005] EWCA Crim 824, [2005] 2 Cr App R 21, [10].

6 *Tirnaveanu* [2007] EWCA Crim 1239, [2007] 2 Cr App R 23, [28], citing *Chalkley & Jeffries* [1998] QB 848.

Malone the Court of Appeal held that a s.78 ruling could be substituted for a missing s.101(3) ruling.[7]

In any case, *Hanson* does not tell us that s.78 no longer applies to any of the s.101(1) gateways. Other cases have since gone further. In *Highton* the Court of Appeal suggested, *obiter*, that s.78 applies to all of the s.101 gateways, a step that also allows the courts to avoid any risk of failing to comply with Article 6 of the European Convention on Human Rights.[8] "*[I]t is right that we should say that, without having heard full argument, our inclination is to say that s.78 provides an additional protection to a defendant.*"

This suggestion was given validity in *O'Dowd*, where the Court of Appeal said that s.78 also applies in the bad character context, and expressed doubt that this was even a "*controversial*" question any more.[9] A number of cases have since been very confident that s.78 should be applied when s.101(3) does not apply,[10] or even in conjunction with s.101(3).[11] Thus

7 *Malone* [2006] EWCA Crim 1860, [50].

8 *Highton* [2005] EWCA Crim 1985, [2006] 1 Cr App R 7, [13]-[14].

9 *O'Dowd* [2009] EWCA Crim 905, [2009] 2 Cr App R 16, [31].

10 *Edwards and Rowlands* [2005] EWCA Crim 3244, [2006] 2 Cr App R 4, [78] seems to assume that s.78 will apply if s.101(3) does not.

11 *Mustapha* [2007] EWCA Crim 1702, [22]: "*It is common ground that in addition to s.101(3) the court may consider the provisions of s.78 of PACE when deciding whether or not to rule evidence of bad character admissible*"; *Murphy* [2006] EWCA Crim 3408 (applied both s.101(3) and s.78); *Tirnaveanu* [2007] EWCA Crim 1239, [2007] 2 Cr App R 23, [27] (where s.101(3) cannot be relied on, use s.78).

it can be used in both gateway (c)[12] and gateway (f)[13] circumstances. It can be used when multiple gateways are being relied upon, and for a mixture of bad character and non-bad character evidence, as in *Fox*: "*Were the evidence admissible under (d) the judge would have had to consider s.101(3). Furthermore, s.78 … was also relevant when considering the cumulative effect of admitting more than one of the three categories of evidence*".[14]

A successful prosecution application to admit non-defendant bad character evidence under s.100 can still be subject to s.78.[15]

Therefore, the prudent view is likely to be that the court can and should apply s.78 in all bad character cases when there is any uncertainty as to the effect of the evidence on the fairness of the proceedings.

---

12 *Bahaji* [2009] EWCA Crim 2863, [35] seems to assume that s.78 applies in gateway (c) circumstances. *Darnley* [2012] EWCA Crim 1148, [33] is probably incorrect in assuming that because s.101(3) does not apply to gateway (c), there is therefore no discretion to exclude evidence falling within that gateway. Section 78 would still apply as the prosecution adduced the evidence.

13 See, e.g., *Hickinbottom* [2012] EWCA Crim 783; *Weir* [2005] EWCA Crim 2866, [2006] 1 Cr App R 19, [44] (s.78 applied in gateway (f) circumstance (but did not help in that case)); *RB* [2008] EWCA Crim 1850, [33]; *Wylie* [2010] EWCA Crim 3110, [16] (seems to accept that s.78 could apply to gateway (f) but would not have helped in this particular case). In *Chrysostomou* [2010] EWCA Crim 1403 the choice was between gateways (g) and (f): "*Our conclusion above that the proper gateway in this case was only that in section 101(1)(g) means that we must focus on section 101(3) rather than section 78 of PACE 1984*" at [39]. However, this must by implication mean that if the proper gateway had been (f), s.78 would have applied.

14 *Fox* [2009] EWCA Crim 653, [28].

15 See *Boxall* [2020] EWCA Crim 688.

5.2.2 Section 78 And Co-Defendants

Section 78 also has a role to play in the event that D2 wishes to object to the admission (at the prosecution's behest) of evidence of D1's bad character.

The wording of s.101(3) and s.103(3) would seem to preclude D2 making any representations under those provisions.

Section 101(3) requires "*application by the defendant*", which must mean the defendant to whom the bad character in s.101 applies. Possibly, if D1 applies to exclude, D2 could then make representations as to the "*adverse effect on the fairness of the proceedings*".

Section 103(3) refers specifically to "*the case of a particular defendant ... unjust for it to apply* in his case." The court would appear to be precluded from considering any unjustness in the case of a defendant who is not the relevant defendant under s.103.

This leaves s.78 which is broad enough to encompass any prosecution evidence, does not require any party's application, and requires the court to look at the whole of the case including the effect on any co-defendants.

Section 78 of PACE may operate to exclude D2's guilty plea to the same offence. The principle in the pre-CJA case of *O'Connor* has been approved in subsequent cases.[16] D1 was tried for conspiracy. D2's guilty plea to the same offence was admitted, allowing the prosecution to rely on an untested statement which had been made by D2 in D1's absence. The Court said:

---

16 *O'Connor* (1987) 85 Cr App R 298, 302-303. See *Smith* [2007] EWCA Crim 2105, and the line of cases following it: *Stevens* [2020] EWCA Crim 280; *D* [2009] EWCA Crim 1361; *M v Uxbridge Magistrates' Court* [2010] EWHC 673 (Admin); *O'Brien* [2016] EWCA Crim 698; *Horne* [2020] EWCA Crim 487. As to the use of s.74 and s.98(a), see Chapter 2.

> "*We find this a difficult point, and, without deciding the full scope of section 74 [for which now substitute s.98(a)], for the purposes of this case, it is sufficient to say that if it was appropriate within the section to admit the conviction of [the co-accused] in the proceedings, we take the view that it would have resulted in a very unfair state of affairs. … section 78 ought to have been brought into play by the learned judge. This was a case in which the admission of the evidence would have such an adverse effect on the fairness of the proceedings that the court ought not to have admitted it.*"

The decision will depend on the facts, but it is suggested that there must be a compelling reason to admit such evidence. Conspiracy cases merit particular care.[17]

5.3 Sections 101(3) And 103(3)

Section 101(3) provides an exclusion for gateways (d) and (g). It is duplicated, in a narrower fashion, for gateway (d) by s.103(3), but only where s.103(2) is being used.

These sections are not applicable to any other gateway.

Summary:

- Concepts of fairness and injustice in the exclusions are intended to guide the conclusion of the trial to a fair outcome. It is in all parties' interests that, if evidence of the defendant's bad character is to be used, that use should result in a fair conviction.

---

17 The appeal was allowed in *Horne* [2020] EWCA Crim 487 because the wrongful admission of the co-defendant's plea to conspiracy "*would have tended significantly to close down the central issue relevant to this count*".

- The pre-CJA test that weighs the probative value of evidence against its prejudicial effect is not strictly applicable, but can be useful.

- There is no set rule about how long is too long between bad character evidence and the present offence.

- Broader principles about the lapse of time can apply to s.78 and other gateways as well.

- A very old conviction may still be admissible if something has happened between that conviction and the index offence that continues the propensity.

- Evidence of bad character that occurred *after* the present matter can also provide sufficient continuity to avoid s.101(3).

5.3.1 Preliminary Observations

What is "*fairness*" in s.101(3) and s.78?[18]

This is not as simple as fairness to both defence and prosecution. In *Tully and Wood* the judge allowed, and even encouraged, the admission of offences dating from when the defendant was 13 years old, because although they would be prejudicial, "*[f]airness, of course, involves fairness to both defence and to the prosecution.*"[19]

The Court of Appeal was critical of this approach, holding that the admission of this wide range of offences did threaten the fairness of the trial.

---

18 Section 103(3) refers not to fairness but to the injustice of allowing similar convictions to be used to establish the defendant's propensity to commit offences of the kind charged. It is possible that the same argument may be made in relation to the assessment of such injustice.

19 *Tully and Wood* [2006] EWCA Crim 2270, [20]. See also *Miller* [2009] EWCA Crim 2890.

It is not enough to say that it is fair to the prosecution to admit the evidence because causing prejudice to the defendant is an accepted consequence of admitting bad character evidence and one that Parliament intended.

In addition, it might even be said that s.101(3) and s.78 are only concerned with adverse effects on fairness from the point of view of the defendant. The language focuses upon adverse effects caused by *admission of prosecution evidence*: such evidence is normally adduced against the defendant, and thus the adverse effect would manifest in unfairness to the defendant.

Fairness is an overall assessment of the trial: it is in the interests of justice (not in the interests of only one party) to ensure that the proceedings, and any conviction, are fair. It is in all parties' interests that, if evidence of the defendant's bad character is to be used, that use should result in a fair conviction. This applies equally to s.78 and s.101(3):

> "*It is well settled that the burden of proof has no part to play in that exercise in relation to Section 78 … The same must apply in relation to Section 101(3) of the 2003 Act. The judge must consider the issue of fairness in the round taking into account the interests of both sides.*"[20]

Do s.101(3), s.78, or s.103(3) include the pre-CJA test that weighs the probative value of evidence against its prejudicial effect?

They do not use the same words,[21] but the test is often still referred to, especially in the s.101(3) context.[22]

---

20 *Shinn* [2023] EWCA Crim 493, [52].

21 See also *Weir* [2005] EWCA Crim 2866, [2006] 1 Cr App R 19, [36].

22 E.g. *Mustapha* [2007] EWCA Crim 1702; *Adams* [2006] EWCA Crim 2013.

The Court of Appeal has said, "*[t]he purpose of the subsection [101(3)] is to ensure that evidence of bad character is not admitted unless it has sufficient probative value to outweigh any risk of prejudice to the defendant and does not affect the fundamental fairness of the proceedings.*"[23]

Prejudicial effect is what arises when evidence, particularly bad character evidence, is given *more* weight than it deserves. If the evidence is capable of enough logical and unemotional force—or probative value—then it should be used in that way, and will by definition not have an *unfair* adverse effect, and hence no prejudicial effect. In reality, it is impossible to know what weight the jury will give to bad character evidence. If it is of a particularly repellent kind, the jury may unconsciously feel that the defendant deserves some punishment, regardless of the probative value of the evidence.[24]

In general, as probative value increases, so too does prejudicial effect against the defendant. When the fairness of the proceedings is at risk, it is likely that the prejudicial effect of the evidence is too great.

Note that, where cross-admissibility is concerned,[25] the exception in s.101(3) cannot apply, because the effect would be to exclude the evidence in question from the trial and create a severed indictment. For the same reason, presumably s.103(3) and s.78 cannot apply (although s.78 can still apply on general grounds).

Section 103(3) is very specific in its application and is not capable of responding to the 'unjustness' of any usage that is not triggered by sub-s 103(1)(a) and 103(2). That is, if conviction bad character evidence is being used to establish the defendant's propensity to commit offences of the kind with which he is charged, then s.103(3) may apply specifically

---

23 *Cortes Plaza* [2013] EWCA Crim 501, [26].

24 Known as "*forbidden reasoning*" or "*just deserts*" reasoning: see *DF* [2011] EWCA Crim 2168.

25 See Chapter 6.

to that method of establishing the propensity, but it will not apply to any other method or any usage other than establishing this propensity. As such it actually provides little protection.

Where bad character evidence has been excluded, it is nonetheless possible for reference to be made to it especially if it is closely linked to other material that is properly the subject of questioning. In *Bernard-Sewell*, although the judge had excluded pursuant to s.101(3) evidence of D's drug dealing, in cross-examination he stated that he had two mobile phones because he was dealing drugs at the time. That answer was not one that the prosecutor had expected. In due course the jury were directed that if they thought the evidence was or may be relevant to the issue of why D had two phones, "*they were to take it into account in his favour*". On appeal, D argued that the prosecutor's questions were inappropriately framed, as they placed D in an impossible position where he would almost inevitably have to admit he was a drug dealer. The jury already had gang evidence which established that drugs supply was a well-recognised aspect of gang criminality. This meant that the "evidence about the drugs phone supported the prosecution case that he was a driving force in the gang and thus a directing mind of the murder."[26]

The Court of Appeal disagreed. The questions asked in cross-examination were appropriate and D could have given "*any number of other reasons for having a second phone*". Any prejudice was addressed by appropriate directions.

> "*There is a difference between being told that the defendant has criminal convictions for conspiracy to supply Class A drugs, and the defendant suggesting that on the day in question he was, or may have been, engaged in street dealing, rather than in plotting a murder.*"

26 *Bernard-Sewell* [2022] EWCA Crim 197, [23].

5.3.2 Time: The General Principle

Time is a key principle in exclusion arguments.

There is no set rule for how long is too long. Case examples vary considerably.

Hanson generally regards the commission date "*of more significance than the date of conviction when assessing admissibility*".[27]

In *Adams* a time gap of 17 years (six years since conviction) was not obviously accounted for in the judge's reasoning. Approving an "*economical*"[28] trial judgment, the Court of Appeal did not summarise the judge's reasons for refusing to exclude the evidence, and it is not evident from the appeal judgment that the judge cited ss.101(3) and (4) or s.103(3). Indeed it would seem that the judge substituted for those provisions a "*familiar balancing exercise*" between probative value and prejudicial effect, a test that does not appear in the Act.

Contrast this with *Dhooper,* where the judge's failure to cite s.101(4) when refusing to exclude evidence of a 13-year-old conviction led to the appeal being allowed. The Court of Appeal said that although there was a possibility the judge had in mind s.101(4), this was not enough.

> *"S.101(4) is an important provision ... It is essential for a court to have regard to the length of time particularly in cases where it is substantial ... Moreover, it is not sufficient for a judge simply to state baldly that he or she has had regard to the length of the interval of time, in a case where the interval is a long one and where the risk that it will have an adverse effect on fairness may be a real one. ... There was plainly a real risk in the present case that the length of time of 13 years would have such an effect. If the judge was proposing nevertheless to admit the evidence, he had to grapple with the length*

Hanson [2005] EWCA Crim 824, [2005] 2 Cr App R 21, [11].

28 *Adams* [2006] EWCA Crim 2013, [12].

> *of time and explain why, despite the passage of 13 years, admission of the evidence would nevertheless not have an adverse effect on the fairness of the proceedings."*[29]

The Court of Appeal begins from the position that to admit the evidence will be problematic, and requires rigorous proof of any reasoning leading to a different conclusion.

It may be helpful to look to the underlying reason for the passage of time exclusion.

The point of interest is not time *per se*, but time *plus* opportunity. For example, two similar events (the first being an offence for which the defendant was convicted, and the second the subject of the present charge) committed five years apart may be treated one way if the offender spent the intervening period in prison, but another way if he spent it in freedom in the community.[30] Of course, any benefits from the period of time in prison should be taken into account as well, for example the possibility of rehabilitation, reform and the likelihood of reoffending. The effect of the time gap also depends upon the type of crime the defendant is accused of having a propensity to commit. If the crime is incest, it is usually easy to identify a lack of opportunity, especially if the defendant has been in prison. But if it involves theft, assault or drug offences, the court should consider the opportunities the defendant had to commit further crimes in prison (where such crimes can be rife), and whether the defendant was involved in these or not. It could even be argued that courts should take into account the potential while imprisoned to become introduced to organised crime and further means of committing crimes.

In *Windsor*, D was charged with conspiracy to cheat the Revenue. The bad character evidence was a previous conviction for cheating the

---

29 *Dhooper* [2008] EWCA Crim 2892, [19].

30 The time gap in *Jackson* [2007] EWCA Crim 1892 might have been addressed in this fashion.

Revenue with the same co-defendants, 14 years before these offences were committed, albeit D had performed a different role in the earlier offending. It was plainly admissible, showing a propensity to commit offences of this type along with the other defendants. It did not fall to be excluded despite the 14-year gap.[31]

Non-conviction bad character evidence is certainly very unlikely to pass s.101(3) and (4) if it is more than 20 years old.[32]

The question of time may be interpreted differently in different gateways.

Gateway (c). As observed in Chapter 4, temporally distant evidence will not usually satisfy gateway (c). In *O*, evidence dated six months before the event charged was not too remote for gateway (d) purposes, but would have been unlikely to satisfy gateway (c).[33]

In the context of gateway (c) it need only be observed that the question whether evidence B can provide a sufficiently valuable explanation for evidence A can often be influenced by the comparative ages of each piece of evidence. This is not *always* true, for a vital explanation may originate in events taking place many years earlier. Time, therefore, is an incidental consideration for the purposes of gateway (c). As was said in *Davis*:

> *"It will be observed that admission under gateway (d), where it is disputed, requires the court to consider the effect on the fairness of the proceedings, in particular by reference to the age of the bad character in question. Such considerations do not apply to gateway (c). That is because its legitimacy is established by reference to its own rationale*

31 *Windsor* [2024] EWCA Crim 798.

32 *Davis* [2008] EWCA Crim 1156, [2009] 2 Cr App R 17.

33 *O* [2010] EWCA Crim 2985. The judge appeared to be answering a prosecution application under gateway (c), but did not consider that the length of time was a factor. The Court of Appeal doubted whether (c) was the correct gateway, and preferred (d), but held that s.101(3) would not have barred admission.

> *and purpose, that is to say the necessity for such evidence, since without it the jury would find it 'impossible or difficult' properly to understand other evidence in the case. The additional requirement, that its value for understanding the case as a whole is substantial, is a further hurdle for its admissibility."*[34]

Of course, gateway (c) is still subject to considerations of fairness overall, as a matter of general principle and by virtue of s.78.

Gateway (e). While ss 101(3) and (4) cannot apply to gateway (e), the Court of Appeal has indicated that the passage of time between a previous conviction and the offence charged may nonetheless "*be a very relevant matter to which the judge should draw attention when he sums up to the jury.*"[35]

Gateway (f). This does not seem to have been the subject of a time-related argument. A possible explanation is that s.105(1)(b) and s.105(3) provide different, but adequate, limitation, and the evidence is less likely to have specific probative value in correcting a false impression if the evidence is very old. Section 78 applies in general.

Gateways (d) and (g).

There are very few gateway (g) cases in which a time-related argument has been mounted. As in so many other arenas, gateway (d) takes centre stage here. However, much of the following discussion is theoretically applicable to gateway (g) cases as well, because the legislative pathway for the two gateways is identical in respect of s.101(3).

The only guidance on what length of time is enough to justify exclusion comes from the main tests for exclusion in s.101(3) and s.103(3), which are not tailored to concepts of time. Each provision only *includes* length

---

34 *Davis* [2008] EWCA Crim 1156, [2009] 2 Cr App R 17, [21].

35 *Edwards and Rowlands* [2005] EWCA Crim 3244, [2006] 2 Cr App R 4, [26].

of time as a factor that may cause the exclusionary mechanism to come into effect. Section 101(3) requires the evidence to have "*such an adverse effect on the fairness of the proceedings*". Section 103(3) requires that "*it would be unjust*" for the bad character evidence to be used to establish the defendant's propensity under s.103(1)(a). Section 103(3) is naturally narrower than s.101(3). Thus, while s.101(3) and (4) in particular, and s.103(3) to a lesser extent, appear to be mandatory exclusions, the interpretation of "*such an adverse effect on fairness*", "*length of time*", and "*unjust*" leaves much to the judge's discretion.[36]

A general principle is clear from *Hanson*: the passage of time does not necessarily diminish the value of bad character evidence,[37] but old convictions are likely to trigger s.101(3) unless they can show a continuing propensity.[38]

This calculation overlaps in gateway (d) cases with the first question of *Hanson*: does the history of conviction(s) establish a propensity to commit offences of the kind charged?

In *McGarvie*, the bad character evidence consisted of rape and attempted rape convictions that occurred 33 years and 18 years before a trial for rape in 2010. The Court, quashing the conviction, said: "*in our judgment, the lapse of time, 32 years since the earlier offences and 18 years since the later*

---

36 Opportunities to deal with "*length of time*" include *Ullah* [2006] EWCA Crim 2003; *Jordan* [2009] EWCA Crim 953 (admitting 18-year-old foreign convictions); *BLW, RAH* [2010] EWCA Crim 1738.

37 *Hanson* [2005] EWCA Crim 824, [2005] 2 Cr App R 21, [49], referring to the defendant's "*sexual mores and motivations*". This is evident in *Morgan* [2009] EWCA Crim 2705, where convictions were admitted despite being at least 20 years old.

38 *Hanson* [2005] EWCA Crim 824, [2005] 2 Cr App R 21, [11]. A period of two years since the conviction is not generally long enough, even for a young defendant: *Ceka* [2012] EWCA Crim 49. However, in *Maitland* [2005] EWCA Crim 2145 the Court excluded non-conviction bad character evidence which was 21 months old.

offence, was considerably too long to permit the admission of the convictions."[39] For the opposite result, see *Gillings*, where eight sexual-assault-related convictions between 1967 and 1988 were admissible at the defendant's trial in respect of rape occurring in 2017 (a gap of 50 to 29 years). The Court said: "*This may have been an extreme case so far as the age of the convictions is concerned, but it is impossible to say that the judge's conclusions were wrong.*"[40]

The same result occurred in *Richards*, where the trial judge admitted evidence of the defendant's convictions for two indecent assaults committed when he was 14-15 years old upon girls aged 12-16. The present offending concerned alleged rapes committed against his partner in 2018-2019 when the defendant was aged 39-40. It appears that C had not wished to support a prosecution, but changed her mind after disclosure of the previous convictions for sexual offences. The judge said, and the Court of Appeal agreed,

> "*I am satisfied that the evidence of the convictions individually and together are capable of demonstrating the propensity the prosecution suggest. I have considered the gap in time. Because there were two incidents of sexual violence at a young age, I am satisfied that this behaviour was not a one-off, but was because of a propensity or is certainly capable of being judged as being so. If so, it is the type of propensity that endures and therefore, despite the gap between those convictions and these allegations, I am satisfied that the propensity is capable of being demonstrated.*"[41]

39 *McGarvie* [2011] EWCA Crim 1414, [18].

40 *Gillings* [2019] EWCA Crim 1834, [2020] 2 Cr App R 8, [33].

41 *Richards* [2022] EWCA Crim 1470, [24].

In *Murphy*, the Court of Appeal did not accept that a conviction for possession of a sawn-off shotgun 20 years earlier was capable of establishing a current propensity to commit firearms offences:

> *"There may be cases where the factual circumstances of just one conviction, even as long ago as 20 years earlier, might be relevant to showing propensity, but we would expect such cases to be rare and to be ones where the earlier conviction showed some very special and distinctive feature, such as a predilection on the part of the defendant for a highly unusual form of sexual activity, or some arcane or highly specialised knowledge relevant to the present offence."*[42]

But, in the similar case of *S*, the Court reached a different result. The defendant was convicted of robbery and of the production of a firearm, or imitation firearm, with intent to commit that robbery. Although the Court quashed the conviction for separate reasons, a secondary issue was the admission of the defendant's previous convictions (presumably under gateway (d)). There were recent convictions for a number of thefts as well as a 1988 conviction for conspiracy to rob which had involved the possession of a firearm.[43] The Court of Appeal distinguished *Murphy*:

> *"Whilst we can see that different views might be taken … about the admission of the old conviction of conspiracy to rob and possession of a firearm in the present case, it is perfectly plain to us that the situation in* Murphy *was different to this case. This was a defendant of whom it could properly be said his convictions demonstrated a propensity to steal and to use violence where necessary."*[44]

---

42 *Murphy* [2006] EWCA Crim 3408, [16]-17].

43 *Smith* [2007] EWCA Crim 2105, [29].

44 *Smith* [2007] EWCA Crim 2105, [30]. *Sully* [2007] EWCA Crim 3512 also distinguished the *Murphy* principle because it only refers to limitations on using one old conviction. In *Sully* there were two, both for indecent assaults on young girls in 1968 and 1974, which were similar enough to the present 2006 offence to be put before the jury. However, the time

This seems to be merely a matter of individual judicial discretion, unless it is really meant to be a demonstration of the intervening event principle discussed next.

5.3.3 The Intervening Event

A very old conviction may still be admissible if something has happened between that conviction and the index offence that continues the propensity.

Per the Court of Appeal in *Murphy*:

> *"In cases with less distinctive features in common, one would require some evidence of the propensity manifesting itself during the intervening period in order to render the earlier evidence admissible as evidence of a continuing propensity."*[45]

In *Cushing*, a 1989 conviction was admissible under s.103(1)(a) only because there was a similar conviction in 2004.[46] Both convictions were together capable of showing a propensity to commit the present offence of robbery. However, given that the *present* offence was also committed in 2004, it may be questioned whether the earlier 2004 conviction could really be "*evidence of propensity … during the intervening period*" and thus establish "*continuing propensity.*" Arguably, it comes too close to the present offence and too far away from the 1989 conviction. Of course, the 2004 conviction could have been admitted alone.

An easier example is *Harding*, where the Court of Appeal said that the *details* of some 1989 convictions were not significant at all, but that the convictions themselves, together with an offence committed in 1996,

---

gap (during which D had not committed any offences) was a factor in the Court of Appeal's decision to reduce sentence.

45 *Murphy* [2006] EWCA Crim 3408, [16].

46 *Cushing* [2006] EWCA Crim 1221.

"*established a propensity to rob*" in 2009.[47] In *Powell*, a manslaughter in 2005 (when D was aged 17), might not by itself have been admitted at a trial for manslaughter in 2014, but when taken with two ABH offences in 2008 and 2012, established a pattern of violent offending that meant all three convictions were admissible.[48]

Caution should be exercised so as not to inadvertently bolster a weak case with bad character evidence. See, for example, *Jackson*, where a 1979 conviction and a 1989-1997 allegation were permitted as bad character evidence in respect of a 2006 trial.[49]

5.3.4 Retrospectivity

Evidence of bad character that occurred *after* the present matter can also provide sufficient continuity to avoid s.101(3).[50]

In *A*, a former police officer was convicted in 2008 of various sexual offences against his daughter. The events had taken place between 1981 and 1992, before his daughter turned 18. The bad character evidence, admitted via gateway (d), concerned D's guilty plea in 2008 to making and distributing indecent photographs of children between 2005 and 2008. The judge restricted use of the conviction and the photographs to material referable to incest, and excluded the actual photos so as to reduce any prejudicial effect. He said s.101(3) was not triggered because although the material was prejudicial, it was highly relevant and powerful.

---

47 *Harding* [2010] EWCA Crim 2145, [13].

48 *Powell* [2015] EWCA Crim 2200, [11]-[18].

49 *Jackson* [2007] EWCA Crim 1892.

50 E.g. *Norris* [2013] EWCA Crim 712 (bad character evidence that occurred 20 months after the incident). See also *Richards* [2018] EWCA Crim 2374; *Adenusi* [2006] EWCA Crim 1059; *Saint* [2010] EWCA Crim 1924.

> *"In my judgment, the bad character evidence upon which the Crown seek to rely is so relevant, because it supports the proposition that* at the time the bad character evidence arose the defendant had developed *an entrenched, persistent and sustained interest in sexual offending against children, with a particular preoccupation with father/daughter incestuous sexual activity."*[51]

The prosecution argument was that D's later activity indicated a developing propensity, dating back to the time of the offences against his daughter. It was also relevant that the daughter had made previous complaints to her family while the events were happening, with no knowledge of the other offences that now constituted the bad character evidence. Thus, the judge said:

> *"a reasonable jury would be entitled to consider the complainant's independent complaint and assess it in the light of the defendant's subsequent computer misuse, and conclude that the proposition that the complainant should make her complaints against an innocent man who just happened later in life to develop peculiar sexual preoccupations consistent with the complainant's complaint is profoundly unlikely."*[52]

The Court of Appeal said that incest was so abnormal and the scope of victims so narrow that the time gap was not as significant as it might be in other cases.[53] D argued that if the daughter had complained immediately, the bad character evidence would not have existed at that time and so could not have prejudiced the trial. The Court of Appeal held that the judge had considered this argument under s.101(3), and, as his decision

51 *A* [2009] EWCA Crim 513, [16] (emphasis added).

52 *A* [2009] EWCA Crim 513, [17].

53 *A* [2009] EWCA Crim 513, [20].

was not plainly wrong or *Wednesbury* unreasonable, appellate interference was precluded.[54]

Thus, guidelines for the treatment of retrospectivity might look something like this:

1. In general, a time gap of more than 20 years between the (alleged) commission of each offence points strongly towards exclusion under s.101(3) (and s.103(3)). The smaller the time gap (on either side of the present events), the less problematic it is to attribute a propensity to D at the time of the present events.

2. The time gap may be of less significance (although the court must have regard to it by the wording of sub-sections 101(3) and (4)) when the nature of the bad character evidence is so unusual that it requires the existence of special circumstances. Incest is a common example of the need for special circumstances.[55]

3. In general, *subsequent* bad character evidence, while less common, is no less admissible under the CJA. There are no temporal limits in the legislation. Nonetheless, the weight of events happening 20-25 years *after* the events in question will be very low.

4. Character is essentially the same throughout one's lifetime (barring some altering event that can be proved). In general, therefore, a person's character can be the same 25 years before the event as it is 25 years after that event. The result of this in *A* may be broadly correct, because of the type of offence concerned, but in general taking this reasoning to its logical conclusion suggests that a person is rarely likely to change at all. This is not

54 *A* [2009] EWCA Crim 513, [22], [24].

55 In *D, P and U* [2011] EWCA Crim 1474, [2012] 1 Cr App R 8, [45] the Court of Appeal said, in a slightly broader context, that "*a sexual interest in young children is a characteristic which is unlikely to change over years.*"

categorically true,[56] and any use of propensity reasoning should take account of the possibility of changes in character. The onus of proving that character has not changed should rest with the prosecution, as can be seen in the above cases on intervening events.

5.3.5 Gateway (g) And The Exclusionary Provision

There are very few gateway (g) cases employing s.101(4). This may be due to the lack of purpose that gateway (g) has. Whereas the gateway (d) discussions are principally directed towards the reliability of the bad character evidence in establishing a matter in issue (usually propensity to commit the kind of offence), there is no similarly identifiable reason for limiting evidence admitted via gateway (g).

In *Hearne*, the defendant was convicted of burglary. He had two previous convictions, both for burglary, in 1987 and 1997, 20 and 10 years before the present case, when he was aged 40 and 50 years respectively. In both cases he pleaded guilty. The defendant agreed that gateway (g) was correctly triggered by his assertion that he was not committing burglary but rather rescuing illegally-kept wild birds, which was an attack on the character of C (whose business involved selling valuable birds). However, the defendant then contended that the age of the convictions threatened the fairness of the proceedings and should be excluded under s.101(3) and (4).

The Court of Appeal held that the purpose of admission was not to demonstrate a propensity for untruthfulness, but simply as "*background*", to show the character of the person making the allegations against C.[57]

> *"The offences were, it is true, old. ...[but] It is trite that this court cannot interfere unless the response to the question of whether they*

[56] If it were, efforts in rehabilitation and restorative justice might be said to be futile.

[57] *Hearne* [2009] EWCA Crim 103, [9].

> *should be admitted, or it was unfair to do so was outwith the range of reasonable responses. In our judgment, it was not. Plainly, as [D], fairly accepts, there had been an attack upon the character of [C] and it would have skewed the fairness of the trial had the jury been deprived of the knowledge that the source of those allegations was someone who, at a mature age, had committed burglary."*[58]

That is, "*background*" bad character evidence (especially convictions) of the defendant has no ascertainable time limits. It is not a question of judgment as to whether the evidence is sufficiently probative in some matter, it is simply a question of fact: whether the bad character evidence illustrates the background of the defendant. If it does, the lapse of time does not affect that illustration. The illustration need not be complete, or proportionate, because none of these requirements is part of the elements of gateway (g), unlike (f), (c), or even (d) (for which some amount of relevance needs to be established).

The result is that although the legislation provides a theoretical safeguard in s.101(3) and (4), it is not often activated with respect to gateway (g). As will be seen in the gateway (e) context below, one course of action by the courts in response to unexpectedly weak or non-existent legislative safeguards is to reinforce the strength of the primary legislative test, exercising greater rigour in its interpretation and application.[59] This has not happened in the gateway (g) context, although it would be facilitated by focusing upon the general fairness provision in s.101(3).[60] At the very least, it should be observed here that s.101(4) is intended to apply to gateway (g), and if the case law renders s.101(4) largely ineffective in relation to gateway (g), the reasoning in *Phillips* suggests we should look to

---

58 *Hearne* [2009] EWCA Crim 103, [6]. It would seem that a gap of 10 or 20 years is less significant when the defendant is of mature years, as presumably an older defendant is less likely to change in the intervening time.

59 See *Phillips* [2011] EWCA Crim 2935, [2012] 1 Cr App R 25.

60 As opposed to the particular question of time specified by s.101(4).

other parts of the legislation, such as s.101(3), s.106, and s.101(1)(g) itself, to limit the admission of evidence via gateway (g).[61]

The exclusionary provisions still operate on evidence admitted via the *Highton* route, as to which see Chapter 4 gateway (g).

If evidence admitted via one gateway is later used for another purpose, the exclusionary provisions should be re-examined. The options when exercising s.101(3) or s.78 retrospectively upon the new usage are to (1) direct the jury to ignore the bad character evidence entirely, or (2) direct the jury to use the evidence for specified purposes only, or (3) discharge the jury.[62]

Of course, s.101(3) and s.103(3) are limited by the gateway used. Section 101(3) only applies if gateways (g) or (d) are used.[63] Neither s.101(3) nor s.103(3) can apply in the situation where the gateway is not (d) or (g), even if the usage made of the evidence is one that is traditionally associated with one of those gateways.

To fill this gap, the Court of Appeal in *Highton* relies upon s.78 of PACE. The differences between s.78 and s.101(3) are examined above. Section 78 cannot perform a pseudo-101(3) function for all gateways to which *Highton* may apply. In particular, *Highton* makes no distinction between prosecution gateways and defence gateways, but s.78 does. Therefore, presumably, evidence already admitted at the defendant's behest (e.g. via

---

61 *Nelson* [2006] EWCA Crim 3412 is an example of doing this, using s.101(3) to mitigate the fact that gateway (g) does not require that either the defendant or the attacked person take the stand.

62 *Henderson* [2010] EWCA Crim 1269, [2010] 2 Cr App R 24, [167] is another example of such a direction, in the context of possible gateway (d) usage when the admitting gateway was (c).

63 Note the limited usefulness of s.101(4) for gateway (g) purposes, because whatever the age of the bad character evidence, it still tends to illustrate the defendant's background.

gateways (c) or (e)), can be used by the prosecution for any relevant purpose without activating any protection.[64]

5.4 Gateway (e) And The Ability To Exclude

Summary:

- There is no discretion to exclude evidence admissible under gateway (e).
- However, non-compliance with the Criminal Procedure Rules may be used to effectively 'exclude' such evidence.
- "*Substantial probative value*" means "*an enhanced capability of proving or disproving a matter in issue*".
- In the absence of a statutory limitation upon gateway (e), courts should ensure that the tests within the gateway itself are applied with greater precision and care.
- The assessment of substantial probative value includes the risk that the jury might become distracted from its focus on the present offence by the admission of that evidence.

The judge has no discretion to exclude evidence admitted via gateway (e), even if failure to do so would have an adverse effect on the fairness of the proceedings in respect of one co-defendant.[65]

This "*position in law is consistent with the historic rule that a defendant must be allowed to advance relevant evidence in his or her defence, even if it*

---

64 The Court has expressed "*hope*" that this would not happen: *Robinson* [2005] EWCA Crim 3233, [2006] 1 Cr App R 32.

65 *Land* [2006] EWCA Crim 2856; *Reid* [2006] EWCA Crim 2900, [23]; *Ferdhaus* [2010] EWCA Crim 220, [8].

is damaging to a co-accused."[66] There is also no other residual common law principle that would allow exclusion. "*[T]he discretionary power to exclude relevant evidence which is tendered by the prosecution, if its prejudicial effect outweighs its probative value, does not apply to the position as between co-accused.*"[67]

However, there are ways around this. In *Musone*, the defendant M and co-defendant C were convicted of the murder of a fellow prisoner. A third defendant, S, was acquitted of murder on the judge's direction (but convicted of assisting M). M said that C had committed the murder. C said that he saw M with the deceased in his prison cell just after the stabbing. Both defendants had convictions involving the use of knives, but none for murder.

On the tenth day of the trial, M indicated that he wanted to adduce evidence under gateway (e) that, although acquitted some 12 years previously of an offence of murder, C had admitted (about a year before this trial) to M that in fact C was guilty of that murder.

The judge ruled that the evidence of the confession was admissible under gateway (e). The important matter in issue was whether it was C rather than M who had wielded the knife. The evidence had substantial probative value because the evidence of the confession to murder was evidence which was capable of showing that it was not M who stabbed the victim, but rather C. Since neither defendant had convictions for murder, if the jury accepted that C had confessed to committing murder then that was evidence which could suggest that C had killed the present victim. Moreover, the confession by C contradicted his acquittal, and might have shown a propensity to untruthfulness (s.104(1)). However, the judge held that M's failure to raise the issue earlier meant it must be excluded.

---

66 *L* [2009] EWCA Crim 2688, [25].

67 *Apabhai* [2011] EWCA Crim 917, [27].

The Court of Appeal disagreed with his first reason for excluding the evidence, namely that he had an Article 6 power to ensure a fair trial. There is no express power to exclude evidence admissible under gateway (e).

However, the Court agreed with the second reason that the judge gave for excluding the evidence. Although s.111 of the CJA does not give the court power to prohibit the admission of bad character evidence where the party seeking to admit it has breached a procedural requirement, an equivalent power can be found in the *rules* made under s.111 (now Part 21, r 21.6(1) of the Criminal Procedure Rules 2020).[68] Using this power, the Court held, the judge is allowed to exclude bad character evidence in circumstances where the defendant has deliberately manipulated the trial process so as to give the co-defendant no opportunity of dealing properly with the application (as opposed to delay by mere oversight). The overriding objective of the Criminal Procedure Rules (r 1.1) is that criminal cases be dealt with justly, and each participant in the conduct of each case must conduct the case in accordance with the overriding objective (r 1.2).

> *"In our view it is not possible to see how the overriding objective can be achieved if a court has no power to prevent a deliberate manipulation of the rules by refusing to admit evidence which it is sought to adduce in deliberate breach of those rules."*[69]

Note that a similar point is made in the Crown Court Compendium at 12.1(3): "*When considering the admission of evidence the court must also look to its case management duties ... This will involve consideration of the*

68 *Musone* [2007] EWCA Crim 1237, [2007] 2 Cr App R 29, [56]. At the time, this was the CPR 2005 and the rule worded slightly differently, but the effect is the same and can be achieved today using CPR 2020. See also *Lawson* [2006] EWCA Crim 2572, [2007] 1 Cr App R 11.

69 *Musone* [2007] EWCA Crim 1237, [2007] 2 Cr App R 29, [59].

purpose for which it is proposed to admit evidence of bad character whether by agreement or otherwise before it goes before the jury."[70]

Using the Rules in this way assists the court in meeting the fair trial requirement in Article 6. However, this power should only be used in circumstances where the only way in which the court can ensure fairness is by excluding such evidence. As *Musone* points out, these are unusual circumstances and are not likely to arise often.[71]

The wider consequence of not having a discretion to exclude evidence admitted via gateway (e), is that the gateway itself is susceptible to creative interpretations designed to perform the functions of such a discretion. This can be seen in the interpretation of "*substantial probative value*" (see discussion of *Phillips* and *Dizaei* in Chapter 5 gateway (e)).

The Court of Appeal in *Phillips* made it very clear that under the new CJA scheme,

> *"No such limitation is imposed by the 2003 Act upon applications made under section 100 and section 101(1)(e). For these reasons, it is important, in our view, that sight is not lost of the rigour of the statutory test of substantial probative value upon a matter in issue between the defendants which is of substantial importance in the context of the trial as a whole."*[72]

That is, in the absence of a statutory limitation upon gateway (e), courts should ensure that the tests within the gateway itself are applied with greater precision and care.

---

70 Crown Court Compendium Part I, July 2024.

71 They may have arisen in *Ramirez* [2009] EWCA Crim 1721, [42], where D2 had volunteered, in-chief and without notice, bad character evidence about D1 in support of D2's contention that he was afraid of D1.

72 *Phillips* [2011] EWCA Crim 2935, [2012] 1 Cr App R 25, [40].

Phillips and *Dizaei* make a significant addition to the meaning of "*probative value*". The assessment of evidential probative value has not traditionally been the sphere in which to air concerns about satellite trials. Evidence that, were it to be believed,[73] would have immense probative value may nonetheless demand a satellite trial in order to convince the jury of its truth. This does not prevent it from having probative value. That is why, where prosecution evidence is concerned and an exclusionary provision exists (such as s.101(3) or s.78), the risk of satellite litigation falls to be considered when exercising that exclusionary power, not when deciding admissibility under a relevance-based test. Yet the *Phillips* line of reasoning has, in an effort to provide a substitute-exclusionary power, included such considerations in the test for substantial probative value, at least as regards defence evidence.[74]

5.5 Section 107 Stopping The Case Where Evidence Contaminated

"107 Stopping the case where evidence contaminated

(1) If on a defendant's trial before a judge and jury for an offence—

> *(a) evidence of his bad character has been admitted under any of paragraphs (c) to (g) of section 101(1), and*
>
> *(b) the court is satisfied at any time after the close of the case for the prosecution that—*
>
> > *(i) the evidence is contaminated, and*

[73] Section 109 requires the judge to assume it is true.

[74] Given its focus on the lack of exclusionary provisions for defence evidence, the Court in *Phillips* probably did not intend to suggest modifications to the existing exclusionary provisions for prosecution evidence.

(ii) the contamination is such that, considering the importance of the evidence to the case against the defendant, his conviction of the offence would be unsafe,

the court must either direct the jury to acquit the defendant of the offence or, if it considers that there ought to be a retrial, discharge the jury.

(2) Where—

(a) a jury is directed under subsection (1) to acquit a defendant of an offence, and

(b) the circumstances are such that, apart from this subsection, the defendant could if acquitted of that offence be found guilty of another offence,

the defendant may not be found guilty of that other offence if the court is satisfied as mentioned in subsection (1)(b) in respect of it.

(3) … [duplicate provision concerning a determination under s.4A(2) of the Criminal Procedure (Insanity) Act 1964]

(4) This section does not prejudice any other power a court may have to direct a jury to acquit a person of an offence or to discharge a jury.

(5) For the purposes of this section a person's evidence is contaminated where—

(a) as a result of an agreement or understanding between the person and one or more others, or

(b) as a result of the person being aware of anything alleged by one or more others whose evidence may be, or has been, given in the proceedings,

the evidence is false or misleading in any respect, or is different from what it would otherwise have been."

Key points:

- S.107 applies only to jury trials. It does not apply to summary trials in a magistrates' court or a *Newton* hearing.[75]

- It is in practice very limited.[76] It requires that there be "*a person's evidence*", and that this evidence be contaminated by reason of some influence by persons or evidence given (or which may be given) in the case.

- There is no formal statutory requirement that any party need *apply* for a determination under s.107.[77] As a matter of common sense, the court would be free to make a determination of its own volition; arguably it is obliged to do so if the evidence raises the possibility of contamination.

- The test for stopping the case is whether the conviction would be unsafe—reflecting the test that the Court of Appeal would apply on appeal against conviction.

- The judge has to make a finding of fact[78] as to whether the requisite contamination has occurred. If the judge is not satisfied that it has, s.107 does not apply. However, s.107 does not oblige the judge to make a finding as to contamination when determining admissibility of bad character evidence.[79]

---

75 *Bradley* [2005] EWCA Crim 20, [31].

76 For some of the history and early discussion, see *Lamb* [2007] EWCA Crim 1766.

77 *Woolf* [2011] EWCA Crim 2764, [31].

78 See *BR* [2014] EWCA Crim 1311, [18].

79 *Marke* [2023] EWCA Crim 505, [14].

- If the judge is satisfied, the case must be stopped. There is no discretion.[80] It does not matter that there might otherwise be 'a case to answer' in the *Galbraith* sense.

- By implication, if there is merely a possibility or risk of contamination, this question should properly be left to the jury with appropriate directions.[81] In *BR*,[82] s.107 was not satisfied even though the complainants had had contact with each other and had discussed the defendant and aspects of their allegations. Contact between extended family members who are also complainants, as in this case, is "*quite typical*". The question of collusion or innocent contamination was one for a properly directed jury. The same case suggests that a financial motive or prospect of compensation to complainants does not mean that the evidence given is contaminated.

- The provision can only be used after the prosecution has closed its case.

- Failure formally to treat evidence as bad character evidence (s.107(1)(a)) does not affect the application of s.107.[83] That is, if evidence *should* have been treated as bad character evidence under s.101 gateways (c)-(g), but for whatever reason was not, an argument can still be made under s.107.

- A formal ruling from the judge is required: s.110(2)(c).

---

80 *Card* [2006] EWCA Crim 1079, [2006] 2 Cr App R 28, [22].

81 See Chapter 6 on cross-admissibility.

82 *BR* [2014] EWCA Crim 1311; *N(H)* [2011] EWCA Crim 730; and recently *McCafferty* [2023] EWCA Crim 1650.

83 *Woolf* [2011] EWCA Crim 2764, [31].

The key case on s.107 is *Card* where, unusually, the Court held that s.107 had been satisfied and the jury should have been discharged. In that case, the Court discussed the purpose behind s.107:

> *"to reduce the risk of a conviction based on over-reliance on evidence of previous misconduct and acknowledges the potential danger that, where the evidence is contaminated, the evidence of bad character may have a disproportionate impact on the evaluation of the case by the jury. In other words the dangers inherent in contamination may be obscured by the evidence of the defendant's bad character."*[84]

The successful appeal in *Card* was based on the clear contamination created by the two complainants having discussed their allegations with their mother. There was "*plain and unequivocal evidence that [C1's] evidence was different from what it would otherwise have been as a result of the conversations with her mother*". That evidence had led to a successful submission of no case to answer (second limb) in relation to C1's allegation. However, C2's allegation was left to the jury. But C2 had been present during the same conversation between C1 and the mother. The inference that C2's evidence "*was different from what it would otherwise have been if he had not been present during the same conversation … was virtually inescapable.*" The conviction was quashed.

Card proposes that, if there might be a "*responsible*" suggestion of contamination, it is better to avoid admitting any bad character evidence until the suggested contaminated evidence has been examined at trial.[85] It is unclear how this should work in practice. The wording of s.107(1) suggests that the "*evidence*" in question is the "*evidence of his bad character evidence*", not the evidence in the case more generally. Thus, any allegation of contamination must be about the bad character evidence (the test in s.107(5) would seem to bear this out, as it references coincidence bad

---

[84] *Card* [2006] EWCA Crim 1079, [2006] 2 Cr App R 28, [21]. See also *King* [2008] EWCA Crim 3301.

[85] *Card* [2006] EWCA Crim 1079, [2006] 2 Cr App R 28, [23].

character evidence[86]). It is not clear how the contaminated evidence could be examined at trial without the bad character evidence being admitted as well.

Section 107 is not an excuse for simply repeating arguments against the admissibility of the bad character evidence.[87]

5.6 Section 108 Convictions When A Youth

"108 Offences committed by defendant when a child

(1) Section 16(2) and (3) of the Children and Young Persons Act 1963 (c. 37) (offences committed by person under 14 disregarded for purposes of evidence relating to previous convictions) shall cease to have effect.

(2) In proceedings for an offence committed or alleged to have been committed by the defendant when aged 21 or over, evidence of his conviction for an offence when under the age of 14 is not admissible unless—

> *(a) both of the offences are triable only on indictment, and*
>
> *(b) the court is satisfied that the interests of justice require the evidence to be admissible.*

(2A) Subsection (2B) applies where—

> *(a) the defendant has been convicted of an offence under the law of any country outside England and Wales ('the previous offence'), and*
>
> *(b) the previous offence would constitute an offence under the law of England and Wales ('the corresponding offence') if it were done in*

86 As to which Chapter 6 on cross-admissibility.

87 *Renda* [2005] EWCA Crim 2826, [2006] 1 Cr App R 24, [27].

England and Wales at the time of the proceedings for the offence with which the defendant is now charged.

(2B) For the purposes of subsection (2), the previous offence is to be regarded as triable only on indictment if the corresponding offence is so triable.

(3) Subsection (2) applies in addition to section 101."

Under s.108, convictions occurring before the defendant turned 14 are not admissible against the defendant once he turns 21, unless:

(a) both the previous conviction and the current offence are triable only on indictment, and

(b) the court is satisfied that the interests of justice require the evidence to be admissible.

The purpose of s.108 is not obvious:

> "*Quite what is the rationale behind section 108(2) is not entirely clear to us. … At all events it is possible, perhaps, to deduce that Parliament may have had in mind the period of time which might elapse between the age of 14 and the age of 21: but other than that it is difficult to draw any firm conclusions.*"[88]

In practice, most evidence that is caught by s.108 would also be likely to fall foul of s.101(3).[89]

It would appear that the event which has to have happened prior to the defendant's 14th birthday is the "*conviction for an offence when under that*

88 *Clark* [2014] EWCA Crim 1053, [18].

89 As in *B* [2008] EWCA Crim 1850, [17].

age", not "*an offence* committed *when under that age*". Thus, if the trial took place after the defendant turned 14, s.108 would not apply.[90]

However, for a contrary view see *Assani*: "*where the person in question was under 14* at the date of the earlier incident *but over 21 at the date of the trial in which the earlier incident is potentially admissible, section 108 contains a specific restriction on admissibility*".[91] The Court assumed here that the relevant time is the date of the earlier incident, not the earlier conviction. Similar language is used in *B*, which refers to "*the age of the appellant [D] at the time of the misconduct alleged*".[92]

Although s.108 prima facie applies only to convictions, the Court of Appeal has said that the principle should also apply when a judge is asked to admit evidence of misconduct which is alleged to have occurred at a time when the defendant was under the age of 14.[93]

Regardless, even if s.108 does not apply, it is obviously correct that "*judges in this context will be sensitive to an attempt to rely on previous convictions for offending which occurred when the offender was a child and in particular when the offender was a young child.*"[94]

For an example of admission of a conviction acquired when the defendant was aged 14-16, see *Richards*.[95]

---

90 That is the implication of the language in *Hickinbottom* [2012] EWCA Crim 783, [56], where the focus is on the date of conviction.

91 *Assani* [2008] EWCA Crim 2563, [15] (emphasis added).

92 *B* [2008] EWCA Crim 1850, [13].

93 *B* [2008] EWCA Crim 1850, [12].

94 *Clark* [2014] EWCA Crim 1053, [20]; the sentiment is repeated in *Valencia* [2015] EWCA Crim 857, [19].

95 *Richards* [2022] EWCA Crim 1470.

CHAPTER SIX

JURY DIRECTIONS AND STANDARD OF PROOF

Bad character does not end with the success or failure of an argument on a pre-prepared application. The jury needs to be directed on how to use the evidence.

The Crown Court Compendium, Part 12, sets out the directions on bad character evidence.[1] Directions on cross-admissibility can be found in Part 13. These are not reproduced here.

Bad character directions should be given in writing.[2] They are rarely straightforward enough to be given orally and recollected by jurors.[3]

A split summing up, where directions of law are given in advance of closing speeches, is advisable and is now the norm in all trials.[4]

6.1 Standard Of Proof To Be Satisfied Before Using Bad Character Evidence

Summary:

- The jury must be 'sure' that the bad character evidence is relevant in the way that the prosecution intend it to be used. If the bad

1 Crown Court Compendium Part I, July 2024.

2 Research indicates that written directions are essentially universally welcomed, see, e.g., Professor Cheryl Thomas's work on the subject, summarised in the previous edition of this text.

3 *BQC* [2021] EWCA Crim 1944; *Rashid* [2019] EWCA Crim 2018.

4 *Rashid* [2019] EWCA Crim 2018.

character evidence is not relied upon as demonstrating any relevant propensity, it may be prudent to direct the jury not to use it as such.[5]

- If they are sure, they can use it to support the intended conclusion. They do not have to do so.

- In *Mitchell*-type propensity cases, where there are several instances of misconduct all tending to show a propensity, the jury does not have to be sure that each instance is proved to the criminal standard.

- The test is different when the bad character evidence is relied upon by a defendant. The Compendium wording in this regard has changed from one that explicitly sets out the balance of probabilities ("*to what extent if at all the evidence demonstrates that it is more likely than not that the matter in issue is true*"[6]) and now reads "*to what extent if at all the evidence may demonstrate the matter in issue is true*". However, it is submitted that the same principles apply. Where D2's bad character goes to D1's case, the jury should be directed that they must decide at most on a balance of probabilities (because D1's case must only ever need to be established to that standard). Where the evidence goes to D2's guilt, the "*sure*" test applies (because it is for the prosecution to prove guilt).

- By inference, although it does not appear to be spelled out in the Compendium, where the jury needs to determine the truth of bad character evidence admitted at the defendant's behest and

5 Everson [2021] EWCA Crim 1178, [18].

6 See , e.g., Crown Court Compendium 2020 Part 12.7, compare 2024 version 12.7 para 9(1).

relating to a non-defendant, the standard is the balance of probabilities.[7]

It has never been the case that the jury must be satisfied beyond reasonable doubt of the truth of every single fact upon which they rely in reaching a guilty verdict, nor is it possible to know whether the jury are so satisfied.

Early CJA cases adopted the "*sure*" wording, importing the standard of proof of beyond reasonable doubt.[8] The Court of Appeal in *Vickers* even required that this standard be satisfied for the facts underlying a conviction. Not only should the jury "*be sure*" that the previous convictions demonstrated the propensity in question, but "*they had to be sure about the facts underlying one of those convictions before they acted upon it.*"[9]

In *Ngyuen*, although the Court stated that jurors do not "*all have to travel down the same evidential route*",[10] it was nonetheless necessary that they be satisfied to the criminal standard of proof before relying on bad character evidence as establishing propensity.[11]

The definitive statement is now from the Supreme Court decision in *Mitchell*. That case tells us:

---

7 For an example of an "*inaccurate*" direction, see *Burnett* [2016] EWCA Crim 1941, [48].

8 *Crandle* [2006] EWCA Crim 2663, [30]; *Lafayette* [2008] EWCA Crim 3238, [37]; *Z* [2009] EWCA Crim 20, [2009] 1 Cr App R 34, [27];

9 *Vickers* [2012] EWCA Crim 2689, [37].

10 *Ngyuen* [2008] EWCA Crim 585, [2008] 2 Cr App R 9, [30].

11 *Ngyuen* [2008] EWCA Crim 585, [2008] 2 Cr App R 9, [29].

- The existence of a propensity must be proved to the conventional criminal standard.[12] I.e., the jury need to be sure that the propensity has been proved.

- In *Ngyuen*, the only way in which they could be sure was by being convinced that the sole incident said to show propensity had been proved to the criminal standard.

- However, in cases where there are several instances of misconduct, all tending to show a propensity, the jury do *not* have to be convinced of the truth and accuracy of all aspects of each of those.

- Rather, the jury should allow the individual instances to "*inform*" each other, in assessing whether they are sure propensity exists "*in the round*".

- "*[J]urors are at liberty to follow their own evidential track.*" Individual jurors may be sure that a propensity exists and then take it into account in deciding their individual verdict. The jury as a whole does not need to agree that a propensity exists before some jurors can use it.

It might be said that this standard of proof increases the risk of satellite litigation. *McKenzie* said that proof of previous alleged misconduct (i.e. not via a conviction) "*requires the trial of a collateral or satellite issue*".[13] *Mitchell* states that the avoidance of satellite litigation is one reason for not applying the criminal standard to each instance of bad character.[14] In analysing *O'Dowd*[15] the Supreme Court stated: "*The jury should have been directed to consider whether the sum of that evidence established to the*

---

12 *Mitchell* [2016] UKSC 55, [2017] AC 571, [44].

13 *McKenzie* [2008] EWCA Crim 758, [23].

14 *Mitchell* [2016] UKSC 55, [2017] AC 571, [47].

15 *O'Dowd* [2009] EWCA Crim 905, [2009] 2 Cr App R 16.

criminal standard that the defendant was possessed of the propensity which was alleged. The evidence in relation to those incidents should have been considered cumulatively, not as separate aspects of the case for a propensity, isolated one from the other."[16]

When modifying a good character direction, the Crown Court Compendium states that:[17]

"*where the prosecution relies on disputed evidence of previous misconduct on the part of a defendant otherwise entitled to a good character direction, the judge should direct the jury that:*

> *(1) if they are sure the evidence is true, they may take it into account as evidence of bad character, adding an appropriate bad character direction; whereas*
>
> *(2) if they are not sure the evidence is true, they should disregard it, adding an appropriate good character direction.*"

This direction imports a requirement of "*sure*" into the jury's decision.

A failure properly to direct the jury as to standard of proof is not fatal. In *Dalby*, the Court of Appeal agreed that the judge had failed to give a direction that the jury needed to be sure of the truth of the bad character evidence before they could rely upon it.[18] However, the Court was satisfied that the conviction was safe, because "*the substance of the [bad character] evidence was admitted in the course of the appellant's evidence. That is a significant factor in reducing the impact of the failure to give a direction that the jury needed to be sure of the truth of that evidence before they could*

---

16 *Mitchell* [2016] UKSC 55, [2017] AC 571, [52].

Crown Court Compendium Part I, July 2024, Part 11 paragraph 14. See Chapter 2 for good character.

18 *Dalby* [2012] EWCA Crim 701, [23].

rely upon it."[19] That is, the fact that much of the bad character evidence was accepted by the defendant meant that for practical purposes the jury did not need to make a finding on the truth of those parts, and it was those parts of the evidence that were significant for bad character purposes. This could not, presumably, work if the prosecution was relying upon a part of the evidence that was not agreed.

In *Styles*, even giving a bad character direction where one should not have been given, and failing to give a modified good character direction where it should have been given, was not sufficient to render the conviction unsafe.[20] Contrast *Greenwood*, where in somewhat similar circumstances the conviction was quashed.[21]

There are cases where (along with other successful grounds of appeal) failure to give the correct direction has resulted in a conviction being quashed.[22]

As always, it can be helpful to return to simple first principles, here set out in *MA*:[23]

- First, the judge should identify to the jury in a simple fashion, but clearly, what evidence they were to consider in the way he was about to indicate.

- Secondly, unless they were sure of this evidence, they should discard it. If they were unsure of part of it, they should disregard it and discard it.

---

19 *Dalby* [2012] EWCA Crim 701, [24].

20 *Styles* [2015] EWCA Crim 1619, [35]-[36].

21 *Greenwood* [2012] EWCA Crim 3147, [14].

22 *Hackett* [2019] EWCA Crim 983; *Harty* [2016] EWCA Crim 345.

23 *MA* [2019] EWCA Crim 178, [48]-[54].

- Thirdly, this category of evidence, however admitted, could not amount to direct proof of D's guilt.

- Fourthly, if they were sure of the evidence, or the extent to which they were sure of it, what could it show? Here, a simple direction that it bore on W's relationship to D and his attitudes to her would have sufficed.

- Fifth, if appropriate, a warning against mere prejudice that might arise from the specifics of the bad character evidence (in this case, details that might have arisen from the defendant's faith).

- Sixth, if they accepted all this evidence, it could show it was more likely that the husband would override the lack of consent of the wife.

- Seventh, emphasise any differences or points that undermine the relevance of the bad character evidence (in this case, that one incident came after the last alleged rape).

6.2 The Safety Valve

Summary:

- Jury directions can protect against the erroneous use, or misuse, of bad character evidence: the "*safety valve*".

- Failure to give proper directions is not fatal to a conviction.

In many cases where the judge has or may have made an error in applying the CJA, the Court of Appeal has often relied upon "*safety valve*"[24] of jury directions.

This phrase was first employed in this context in *Eastlake*. Brothers Scott and Nicky were convicted of assault charges. The issue was identification. Bad character evidence about both was admitted via gateway (d): Scott had four convictions relating to street violence between 2003-04; Nicky had a conviction for an assault in 2004, and another for an offence (committed with Scott) in 2004. The defendants' opposition to admission was based on the weakness of the prosecution case, which was based solely upon one witness's identification of the defendants.[25] The Court of Appeal said this was not a weak case, and that in any event the dangers of using bad character evidence in such circumstances were mitigated by jury directions:

> *"This case exemplifies the paradox inherent in the admission of bad character evidence of this sort. The previous convictions were of recent date and for offences similar to (albeit less serious than) those charged in this indictment. The more recent and similar the previous convictions are, the more powerfully they may indicate a relevant propensity; but those factors may strengthen the argument that they should be excluded to avoid the risk of the trial becoming unbalanced by their admission into evidence.*

24 *Eastlake* [2007] EWCA Crim 603, [26]. See also *Culhane* [2006] EWCA Crim 1053; *Isichei* [2006] EWCA Crim 1815; *Osbourne* [2007] EWCA Crim 481; *RR* [2007] EWCA Crim 437; *Saleem* [2007] EWCA Crim 1923; *Tirnaveanu* [2007] EWCA Crim 1239, [2007] 2 Cr App R 23; *Walker* [2007] EWCA Crim 2631, [2008] 2 Cr App R (S) 6; *Lamaletie and Royce* [2008] EWCA Crim 314; *Laurusevicius* [2008] EWCA Crim 3020; *Brisland* [2008] EWCA Crim 2773; *Foster* [2009] EWCA Crim 353; *X* [2012] EWCA Crim 2276.

25 *Eastlake* [2007] EWCA Crim 603, [15].

> *The* safety valve *is of course the giving of proper directions to the jury.*"[26]

The safety valve is therefore another way of dealing with potential unfairness or adverse effect of admitting bad character evidence. It should be approached with caution, because it can skirt a fine line between a case that actually invites exclusion under s.78, s.101(3), or s.103(3), and a case where the evidence is properly admissible but requires clear instructions as to its limitations.[27]

However, the absence of the correct jury direction does not therefore render a conviction *unsafe*.[28] In *Ahmed*[29] the directions were "*scrappy*", but the prosecution case was strong and the previous convictions "*plainly demonstrated a relevant propensity.*"

In *Girma*, evidence of the convictions of non-defendants was admitted via s.74 of PACE (and, wrongly, gateway (c)). The judge "*said he would give a careful direction to the jury that they could not use the convictions to bolster the present case.*"[30] As to the later failure to do this:

> *"In the event, he said nothing about [the convictions]. No-one invited him to do so.*
>
> *"As it seems to us, this is wholly peripheral. It may be (and it is unnecessary to decide) that absent agreement by the defendants, this was*

26 *Eastlake* [2007] EWCA Crim 603, [25]-[26] (emphasis added).

27 See, e.g., the unusual set of events in *Wilson* [2008] EWCA Crim 134, [2008] 2 Cr App R 3.

28 See also *Brisland* [2008] EWCA Crim 2773, [23]. For a failure to direct on usage when the issue is as complex as the cross-admissibility of several counts in the same trial see *Francis-Macrae* [2006] EWCA Crim 2635.

29 *Ahmed* [2011] EWCA Crim 3253, [11].

30 The convictions, of alleged co-offenders, had both positive and negative implications for various defendants in the present trial.

> *irrelevant evidence which should not have been admitted. However, its admission could not conceivably have prejudiced these appellants. It could not conceivably affect the safety of the convictions. We need say no more about it."*[31]

In this case the strength of the evidence meant that the Court was not unduly concerned that non-defendant bad character, admitted via the wrong legislative path, had been left to the jury without direction as to its use or scope.

It might be concluded, therefore, that directions to the jury on the use of bad character evidence are in principle required, in practice useful, but not always necessary. This is so despite the pivotal statement in *Edwards and Rowlands* that jury directions are of "*the first importance*".[32] And, more recently in *Fanta*, the caution:

> "*It remains critical, therefore, that the legal directions ensure that the jury will approach the evidence of bad character correctly, and the courts must be careful not simply to assume that juries will understand the relevance of this kind of evidence in the same way as lawyers and judges. Materially deficient directions, particularly with complex evidence, are likely to lead to the conviction being quashed, depending always on the circumstances of the particular trial.*"[33]

Note that accidental or erroneous reference to bad character can sometimes be remedied by a warning to the jury to ignore the material.[34]

---

31 *Girma* [2009] EWCA Crim 912, [2010] 1 Cr App R (S) 28, [84]-[85]. *Tirnaveanu* [2007] EWCA Crim 1239, [2007] 2 Cr App R 23, [37]. See also *Heron* [2020] EWCA Crim 966.

32 *Edwards and Rowlands* [2005] EWCA Crim 3244, [2006] 2 Cr App R 4.

33 *Fanta* [2021] EWCA Crim 564, [65].

34 *Burchell* [2016] EWCA Crim 1559, [32]; *Kelly* [2015] EWCA Crim 500.

Thus, where proper directions are given they may be capable of saving the day (the safety valve in operation), but if the valve is 'off' the case may nonetheless be safe. Of course, a case may be safe without the operation of the valve—most commonly because the evidence against the defendant was so strong that the jury would nonetheless have convicted.

6.3 Are Juries Influenced By Bad Character Evidence?

The jury's actual use of bad character evidence cannot easily be studied. Nor can the effect of jury directions on the use of that evidence. Some guidance is available by looking at retrials that used different evidence, and research and mock-trials.[35] For an analysis of this please see the first edition of this book.

6.4 Cross-Admissibility

Section 112(2) reads:

"Where a defendant is charged with two or more offences in the same criminal proceedings, this Chapter (except section 101(3)) has effect as if each offence were charged in separate proceedings; and references to the offence with which the defendant is charged are to be read accordingly."

The effect of s.112(2) is that evidence in relation to count 1 on the indictment, and in fact a conviction on count 1 itself, can only be used by the jury in relation to count 2 if count 1 and its evidence satisfy a s.101 gateway.

As a result, the notice provisions apply (see Chapter 2). However, the failure to give notice is not fatal if the defence is not "*taken by surprise*".[36]

---

[35] See, e.g., studies by Sally Lloyd-Bostock and Cheryl Thomas.

[36] *Brennand* [2023] EWCA Crim 1384, [31].

Cross-admissibility must be addressed by the judge with counsel well in advance of any directions and closing speeches. Raising the point on the first day of summing-up is "*not a helpful way to proceed*".[37]

In practice, the cross-admissibility direction is often given as a matter of course. Gateway (d) cross-admissibility generally applies to the following categories:[38]

(1) Coincidence approach. When independent but similar complaints are made against the same person, the jury "*may be permitted to consider the improbability that those complaints are the product of mere coincidence or malice*". This means that C1's evidence on count 1 can be relevant to C2's credibility on count 2. This is an important matter in issue: s.101(1)(d)). Jurors first need to exclude any collusion/innocent contamination between the similar complaints.[39] The judge should identify the similarities and differences to assist the jury.[40]

(2) Propensity approach. The jury may be sure of D's guilt upon count 1, and if, but only if, they are also sure that guilt on count 1 establishes D's propensity to commit that kind of offence, they may proceed to consider whether the propensity makes it more likely that D committed an offence of a similar type alleged in count 2 on the same indictment (evidence of propensity: section 101(1)(d) and section 103(1)(a)).

The first category is described as the "*coincidence approach*". It is effectively what used to be known as "*pooling*" evidence in pre-CJA

---

37 *Gabbai* [2019] EWCA Crim 2287, [2020] 4 WLR 65, [83]-[87]. See also *Adams* [2019] EWCA Crim 1363.

38 *N(H)* [2011] EWCA Crim 730, [31].

39 See, e.g., *Smith* [2017] EWCA Crim 941, [28].

40 Smith [2024] EWCA Crim 342, [42].

commentary. The second category is described as the "*propensity*" approach, which is akin to "*sequential*" evidence in the pre-CJA commentary.

It is rare that both of the above categories will apply to the same counts. In most cases, this would be impermissible bootstrapping: (a) using the similarity of the two complaints on counts 1 and 2 to reach a verdict of guilty on count 1 (the coincidence approach), and then (b) using that guilty verdict to support a guilty finding on count 2 (the propensity approach). The evidence in relation to count 2 having already been used in step (a), it should not be used in step (b) as this would effectively give that evidence twice the weight it should have.

The Court of Appeal has recently indicated that it may be possible to give both directions. This is a matter for the trial judge on the facts of the each case.[41] A glance at the direction given in *Brennand*, and the specimen direction in the Compendium (which has been revised in light of *Brennand*) shows just how difficult it is to prevent double-counting and why this combination should still be used very sparingly. The case of *Smith*, which followed *Brennand*, adopts a more cautious approach:

> *"such directions on cross-admissibility are a potential minefield and call for careful consideration between judge and counsel as to how the direction should be tailored to the facts of the case and whether the jury should be directed on one or both limbs".*[42]

The Court in *Smith* went on to say that although *Brennand* makes clear that the jury can deal with coincidence or propensity first, "*logically the first issue would be to require the jury to be sure that there had been no deliberate or, alternatively, innocent taint of C1 and C2's evidence*".[43] In that case the combination direction was flawed on both coincidence and

---

41 *Brennand* [2023] EWCA Crim 1384, [43].

42 *Smith* [2024] EWCA Crim 342, [36].

43 *Smith* [2024] EWCA Crim 342, [40].

propensity, the effect of which was to render the conviction unsafe. In *BQC*, the conviction was unsafe because of flaws in jury directions including a failure to provide written directions on cross-admissibility or on the combination direction.[44]

Note that the exception in s.101(3) cannot apply, because the effect would be to exclude the evidence in question from the trial and create a severed indictment.[45] For the same reason, presumably s.103(3) and s.78 cannot apply (although s.78 can still apply on general grounds).

For a case where cross-admissibility of different counts should not have been permitted, see *Gabbai*. There, although the relevant counts all alleged rape, they were "*entirely dissimilar*" in the alleged facts and issues in dispute. C1's allegation was based on the removal of a condom during otherwise consensual sex, whilst she was in a relationship with D. C2's allegation was of extreme violence and forced penetration by D, a complete stranger.[46] The prejudicial effect of cross-admissibility in this case was so high that, taken together with other "*aspects of this trial which went awry*", the convictions were unsafe.

Failure to give the cross-admissibility direction is likely to cast doubt on the safety of a conviction. The Court of Appeal in *Adams* issued the following general reminder:

> *"Looking at the matter more broadly, the general tendency of the criminal law over time has been towards a gradual relaxation of rules of evidence and an increasing willingness to trust to the good sense and rationality of juries to judge for themselves whether particular evidence is relevant to an issue they have to decide and if so in what way. But we have not yet reached the point where evidence of a*

---

44 *BQC* [2021] EWCA Crim 1944.

45 For a case where severance and the effect of bad character and cross-admissibility is examined, see *Toner* [2019] EWCA Crim 447.

46 *Gabbai* [2019] EWCA Crim 2287, [2020] 4 WLR 65, [81]-[82].

> *defendant's bad character can be left as a free for all. The particular ways in which evidence that a person has committed one offence may or may not be relevant in deciding whether that person is guilty of another offence are not always immediately obvious even to legal professionals and have had to be worked out by the courts in a number of cases. Lay jurors are entitled to assistance on these questions and cannot be expected to work out the approach which the courts regard as proper for themselves. It therefore seems to us to be essential that, in a case of this kind, the jury should be given clear directions on whether, and if so how, evidence relating to one count may be taken into account in deciding guilt on another count.*[47]

However, this does not mean that in every case in which there is more than one complainant alleging similar offences, the failure to give a cross-admissibility direction will be fatal to the safety of the conviction.[48]

Where there is no reliance on cross admissibility, there is no automatic requirement for a direction in addition to the standard directions on separate consideration of each count.[49]

Wrongful inclusion of a summary charge on the indictment does not necessarily render a conviction on the indictable count unsafe. In *Morris*, the evidence covered by the summary charge was treated as s.98(a) evidence in relation to the indictable counts.[50]

---

47 *Adams* [2019] EWCA Crim 1363, [22].

48 *Ryan* [2021] EWCA Crim 262, [40]. In that case, the failure was fatal and a retrial ordered.

49 *AHC* [2022] EWCA Crim 925, [28].

50 *Morris* [2019] EWCA Crim 147.

CHAPTER SEVEN

CONCLUSION

There is still no straightforward flowchart that covers the application of ss.98-112 and all of the attendant case law. Since the first edition of this book, I have been working on a checklist that might assist.

Preliminary

- When is the best time to decide this issue – now, or at a later stage, and why
- Do the judge and all parties know when it will be determined
- Is all necessary material available to allow a decision to be made

Is the evidence bad character evidence

- First, apply s.112(1) meaning of "misconduct"
- Does s.98(a) or (b) apply to take the evidence out of the CJA regime
  - If so, is the evidence relevant under common law (s.98 not automatically admissible)
  - If neither bad character nor s.98 evidence, revert to common law relevance
- How will the evidence be proved
  - Will it risk satellite litigation
- Consider s.78 for prosecution evidence

- Will its admission trigger other issues e.g. gateway (g)
- How should the jury be directed about the evidence
- Written directions, which should be discussed with the parties

<u>If evidence falls within CJA regime</u>

- Has the appropriate notice/application been made in time
- Consider relevance, starting with s.109 assumption of truth
    - If irrelevant, it is inadmissible
- Who is the subject of the bad character evidence
- Are they a defendant or a non-defendant in these proceedings
    - If a defendant, apply s.108 where relevant
- Consider the specific gateway(s) argued and apply the relevant tests
- How will the bad character be proved
    - Will the bad character evidence be disputed
    - Are facts underlying a conviction being relied upon
    - Will evidence need to be called/tested
    - If risk of satellite litigation or distraction then consider admissibility and exclusions
- Does admission trigger something else, e.g. gateway (g)

- What will happen to the evidence after it is admitted
    - Are there other uses to which it may be put
    - Should these be expressly excluded
    - Are all parties and judge aware of uses/excluded uses
- Do any exclusions apply – especially for gateways (d) or (g)
- Should only part of the evidence be admitted, in particular
    - Gateway (c) – only admit important explanatory evidence, bad character evidence is incidental
    - Gateway (f) – can D withdraw from the false impression? If not, admit only as much as is necessary to correct the false impression.
    - Gateway (g) – entire character need not be admitted, consider why D has attacked someone's character
- Are limitations needed on exploration and use of the evidence so as to balance fairness with effective trial management
- After close of prosecution case, is the evidence contaminated – apply s.107
- How is the jury to be directed on proper and improper uses
- Written directions, which should be discussed with the parties
- At the end, apply s.78 to all prosecution evidence.

Finally, I have retained the following points of 'principle' from the first edition which I consider are always worth asking when embarking on a bad character journey:

- Is it fair to use this evidence in this case?
- Does it distract the parties, the judge, or the jury from the issues that must be resolved in the case?
- Particularly if prosecuting, how does it actually <u>help</u> the tribunal of fact to ascertain the truth (which is not always the same as strengthening the Crown's case theory)?
- If an error is made in respect of the admission or directions on the evidence, how might this affect the safety of any subsequent conviction?

INDEX

MORE BOOKS BY LAW BRIEF PUBLISHING

A selection of our other titles available now:-

'A Practical Guide to Probation Breaches and Other Applications' by Mark Thomas
'A Practical Guide to Remarriage and Divorce' by Cordelia Williams & Claire Howard
'A Practical Guide to Privacy, Transparency, Reporting Restrictions and Closed Proceedings in the Court of Protection' by Laura Mannering
'Beaumont on Barristers – A Guide to Defending Disciplinary Proceedings (Second Edition)' by Marc Beaumont
'A Practical Guide to Payments for Environmental Services' by Ben Sharples
'A Practical Guide to the Law of Pregnancy and Maternity at Work' by Rebecca Thomas
'A Practical Guide to Redundancy – Second Edition' by Philip Hyland & Collette Moore
'A Practical Guide to International Issues for Scottish Family Lawyers' by Susie Mountain, Donna McKay, Ken MacDonald
'A Practical Guide to the Law on Deprivation of Liberty' by Ben Troke
'A Practical Guide to Rights over Airspace and Subsoil – Second Edition' by Daniel Gatty
'A Practical Guide to the Law in Relation to Inquests' by Ramya Nagesh
'A Practical Guide to the Construction and Rectification of Wills and Trust Instruments (Second Edition)' by Edward Hewitt
'A Practical Guide to Data Protection in Social Housing' by Clare Paterson
'A Practical Guide to Spousal Maintenance – Second Edition' by Liz Cowell
'A Practical Guide to International Parental Child Abduction Law (England and Wales)' by Dr Onyója Momoh
'A Practical Guide to Deprivation of British Citizenship' by Sean Ell
'A Practical Guide to Commercial Property Service Charges' by Rachel Garton
'A Practical Guide to Clinical Negligence – Third Edition' by Geoffrey Simpson-Scott (Geoff)
'A Practical Guide to the Rights of Grandparents in Children Proceedings – Second Edition' by Stuart Barlow

'The Electronic Communications Code: A Practical Guide – Second Edition' by Kerry Bretherton KC, James Castle, Mark Loveday
'A Practical Guide to the Independent School Standards – September 2023 Edition' by Sarah McKimm
'A Practical Guide to Estate Administration and Crypto Assets' by Richard Marshall
'A Practical Guide to Parental Alienation in Private and Public Law Children Cases' by Sam King QC & Frankie Shama
'Contested Heritage – Removing Art from Land and Historic Buildings' by Richard Harwood QC, Catherine Dobson, David Sawtell
'The Limits of Separate Legal Personality: When Those Running a Company Can Be Held Personally Liable for Losses Caused to Third Parties Outside of the Company' by Dr Mike Wilkinson
'A Practical Guide to Transgender Law' by Robin Moira White & Nicola Newbegin
'A Practical Guide to 'Stranded Spouses' in Family Law' by Mani Singh Basi
'A Practical Guide to Residential Freehold Conveyancing' by Lorraine Richardson
'A Practical Guide to Pensions on Divorce for Lawyers' by Bryan Scant
'A Practical Guide to Challenging Sham Marriage Allegations in Immigration Law' by Priya Solanki
'A Practical Guide to Digital Communications Evidence in Criminal Law' by Sam Willis
'A Practical Guide to Legal Rights in Scotland' by Sarah-Jane Macdonald
'A Practical Guide to New Build Conveyancing' by Paul Sams & Rebecca East
'A Practical Guide to Inherited Wealth on Divorce' by Hayley Trim
'A Practical Guide to Practice Direction 12J and Domestic Abuse in Private Law Children Proceedings' by Rebecca Cross & Malvika Jaganmohan
'A Practical Guide to Confiscation and Restraint' by Narita Bahra QC, John Carl Townsend, David Winch
'A Practical Guide to the Law of Forests in Scotland' by Philip Buchan
'A Practical Guide to Health and Medical Cases in Immigration Law' by Rebecca Chapman & Miranda Butler
'A Practical Guide to Bad Character Evidence for Criminal Practitioners by Aparna Rao
'A Practical Guide to Extradition Law post-Brexit' by Myles Grandison et al
'A Practical Guide to Hoarding and Mental Health for Housing Lawyers' by Rachel Coyle

'Stephens on Contractual Indemnities' by Richard Stephens
'A Practical Guide to the EU Succession Regulation' by Richard Frimston
'A Practical Guide to Solicitor and Client Costs – Second Edition' by Robin Dunne
'Constructive Dismissal – Practice Pointers and Principles' by Benjimin Burgher
'A Practical Guide to Religion and Belief Discrimination Claims in the Workplace' by Kashif Ali
'A Practical Guide to the Law of Medical Treatment Decisions' by Ben Troke
'Fundamental Dishonesty and QOCS in Personal Injury Proceedings: Law and Practice' by Jake Rowley
'A Practical Guide to the Law in Relation to School Exclusions' by Charlotte Hadfield & Alice de Coverley
'A Practical Guide to Divorce for the Silver Separators' by Karin Walker
'The Right to be Forgotten – The Law and Practical Issues' by Melissa Stock
'A Practical Guide to Planning Law and Rights of Way in National Parks, the Broads and AONBs' by James Maurici QC, James Neill et al
'A Practical Guide to Election Law' by Tom Tabori
'A Practical Guide to the Law in Relation to Surrogacy' by Andrew Powell
'A Practical Guide to Claims Arising from Fatal Accidents – Second Edition' by James Patience
'A Practical Guide to Asbestos Claims' by Jonathan Owen & Gareth McAloon
'A Practical Guide to Stamp Duty Land Tax in England and Northern Ireland' by Suzanne O'Hara
'A Practical Guide to the Law of Farming Partnerships' by Philip Whitcomb
'A Practical Guide to the Law of Unlawful Eviction and Harassment – Second Edition' by Stephanie Lovegrove
'A Practical Guide to Costs in Personal Injury Claims – Second Edition' by Matthew Hoe
'A Practical Guide to the General Data Protection Regulation (GDPR) – Second Edition' by Keith Markham
'A Practical Guide to Working with Litigants in Person and McKenzie Friends in Family Cases' by Stuart Barlow
'Protecting Unregistered Brands: A Practical Guide to the Law of Passing Off' by Lorna Brazell
'A Practical Guide to Secondary Liability and Joint Enterprise Post-Jogee' by Joanne Cecil & James Mehigan

'A Practical Guide to the Pre-Action RTA Claims Protocol for Personal Injury Lawyers' by Antonia Ford

'A Practical Guide to Neighbour Disputes and the Law' by Alexander Walsh

'A Practical Guide to Coercive Control for Legal Practitioners and Victims' by Rachel Horman

'A Practical Guide to the Law of Driverless Cars – Second Edition'

by Alex Glassbrook, Emma Northey & Scarlett Milligan

'A Practical Guide to TOLATA Claims' by Greg Williams

'A Practical Guide to Elderly Law – Second Edition' by Justin Patten

'A Practical Guide to Responding to Housing Disrepair and Unfitness Claims' by Iain Wightwick

'A Practical Guide to the Law of Bullying and Harassment in the Workplace' by Philip Hyland

'How to Be a Freelance Solicitor: A Practical Guide to the SRA-Regulated Freelance Solicitor Model' by Paul Bennett

'A Practical Guide to Prison Injury Claims' by Malcolm Johnson

'A Practical Guide to Advising Clients at the Police Station' by Colin Stephen McKeown-Beaumont

'A Practical Guide to Antisocial Behaviour Injunctions – Second Edition' by Iain Wightwick

'Practical Mediation: A Guide for Mediators, Advocates, Advisers, Lawyers, and Students in Civil, Commercial, Business, Property, Workplace, and Employment Cases' by Jonathan Dingle with John Sephton

'The Mini-Pupillage Workbook' by David Boyle

'A Practical Guide to Crofting Law' by Brian Inkster

'A Practical Guide to the Law of Domain Names and Cybersquatting' by Andrew Clemson

'A Practical Guide to the Law of Gender Pay Gap Reporting' by Harini Iyengar

'NHS Whistleblowing and the Law' by Joseph England

'Employment Law and the Gig Economy' by Nigel Mackay & Annie Powell

'A Practical Guide to Noise Induced Hearing Loss (NIHL) Claims' by Andrew Mckie, Ian Skeate, Gareth McAloon

'An Introduction to Beauty Negligence Claims – A Practical Guide for the Personal Injury Practitioner' by Greg Almond

'Intercompany Agreements for Transfer Pricing Compliance' by Paul Sutton

'Zen and the Art of Mediation' by Martin Plowman

'A Practical Guide to Adoption for Family Lawyers' by Graham Pegg

'A Practical Guide to Industrial Disease Claims' by Andrew Mckie & Ian Skeate
'A Practical Guide to Conducting a Sheriff Court Proof' by Andrew Stevenson
'A Practical Guide to Vicarious Liability' by Mariel Irvine
'A Practical Guide to Applications for Landlord's Consent and Variation of Leases' by Mark Shelton
'A Practical Guide to Relief from Sanctions Post-Mitchell and Denton' by Peter Causton
'A Practical Guide to Equity Release for Advisors' by Paul Sams
'A Practical Guide to Financial Services Claims' by Chris Hegarty
'A Practical Guide to Financial Ombudsman Service Claims' by Adam Temple & Robert Scrivenor
'A Practical Guide to Running Housing Disrepair and Cavity Wall Claims – Second Edition' by Andrew Mckie & Ian Skeate
'A Practical Guide to Holiday Sickness Claims – Second Edition' by Andrew Mckie & Ian Skeate
'Arguments and Tactics for Personal Injury and Clinical Negligence Claims' by Dorian Williams
'A Practical Guide to Drone Law' by Rufus Ballaster, Andrew Firman, Eleanor Clot
'On Experts: CPR35 for Lawyers and Experts' by David Boyle
'An Introduction to Personal Injury Law' by David Boyle